Table of Contents

Executive Summary

During periods of unemployment, whether due to economic downturns, job loss or ongoing barriers to employment, self-employment is a viable means to provide income, assets and other elements of self-sufficiency. The Workforce Investment Act (WIA), which authorizes DOL's American Job Centers (AJCs) (formerly known as One-Stop Career Centers), makes numerous references to self-employment and in fact lists self-employment as an exit outcome for individuals receiving services authorized by WIA.

Congress provided $5,000,000 in the FY 2006 appropriation for the Department of Labor's Office of Disability Employment Policy (ODEP) to develop research-based policy and provide technical assistance to organizations geared toward achieving sustainable self-employment outcomes for individuals with disabilities. Reflecting this, in October 2006 ODEP initiated the Self-Employment Technical Assistance, Resources and Training (START-UP) self-employment program. Four cooperative agreements were awarded to three state or local projects (START-UP/Alaska, START-UP/Florida and START-UP/New York) and one national project (START-UP/USA), which was implemented by a consortium headed by Virginia Commonwealth University (VCU). The goals of each of the three state consortia were to research, test and evaluate innovative models of self-employment service delivery at the sub-national level to determine if those models could be replicated across the country. The goal of the national project was to provide technical assistance to the three state grantees and individuals interested in becoming self-employed, as well as to increase other states' capacity to support potential entrepreneurs with disabilities through information provision and research.

Each state grantee developed a different model for delivering assistance and training to potential entrepreneurs with disabilities. Although these models shared a common goal, they differed in elements such as the partners included in their collaborative work groups, types of training provided to front-line staff, and methods of direct service provision.

START-UP/New York developed a broad network of 55 partners and collaborators, including the program management team; research universities and colleges; financial institutions; disability service agencies at the county, state and national levels; and technology and economic development agencies. New York also used a business incubator, in collaboration with the state vocational rehabilitation (VR) agency and local Small Business Development Center (SBDC), to provide advice and training to program participants, including continued follow-up after business launch. Furthermore, START-UP/New York developed a course, entitled "*Inclusive Entrepreneurship*," which is now being offered through Syracuse University's Whitman School of Management to educate both graduate and undergraduate students about the issues that people with disabilities face when they seek entrepreneurship. Students taking the course are assigned to consulting teams to provide assistance to program participants.

START-UP/Alaska's consortium included the state's VR program, AJCs and SBDCs, among others. Using a customized self-employment model, the program operated three sites based in AJCs and used a Virtual Business Advisor to provide services and support to program participants in remote areas of the state using electronic tools.

START-UP/Florida's consortium included the Florida workforce system (Workforce Florida, Inc. and the Agency for Workforce Innovation), the Agency for Persons with Disabilities and the Department of Education, Division of Vocational Rehabilitation. The program tested three self-employment training models at three sites around the state. One training model was developed by the faculty from Martin County Public Schools, another by the University of South Florida and the third by a nationally recognized entrepreneurial training program. The state VR agency developed and implemented a vendor training and certification program for self-employment. Individuals who successfully completed training became Certified Business and Technical Assistance Consultants.

Even though they faced multiple barriers within their states, all three states exceeded their expectations regarding the number of entrepreneurs who would start businesses. Overall, the states had varied levels of success in developing a self-employment infrastructure and increasing capacity for serving potential entrepreneurs with disabilities.

The national grantee, START-UP/USA, provided intense technical assistance to and collected outcome data from the three state grantees. It also provided technical assistance to individual potential entrepreneurs through its website, webinars, fact sheets and case studies. It reported that several other states requested information about starting their own self-employment programs. To assist, START-UP/USA developed an online training course titled "Overview of Self-Employment for Entrepreneurs with Disabilities," which continues to be available.

Success stories shared by entrepreneurs from the state and national initiatives provide insight into the issues and methods used to assist them in starting a business. Furthermore, policy and system barriers arose that were both expected and unexpected as the initiative began. Expected barriers included negative attitudes and views of service providers, lack of technical knowledge of program participants, inconsistent performance expectations, policies that created financial disincentives, complicated work incentives and funding challenges. Unexpected challenges included views and attitudes from the participants (jobseekers with disabilities) as well as language and communication.

Recommendations developed in response to the barriers experienced by the grantees during the period of the grants address policy alignment, cross-system collaboration and public-private sector investment.

This report is intended to help policy makers, workforce development professionals and people with disabilities view self-employment as a viable source of income for people with disabilities. With adherence to recommendations and support from all stakeholders both within the varying levels of government as well as community partners, individuals with disabilities can successfully start and maintain their own businesses and reap the benefits of self-employment.

1. INTRODUCTION

Background

1. Self-Employment

Many Americans are the descendants of people who came to the United States from across the globe to realize opportunity and exercise freedom. Steeped in the spirit of independence, the earliest Americans were self-employed, primarily in agriculture. However, as the nation's economic base shifted from farming to manufacturing and then on to the "Information Age," the nature of employment in America did as well, with wage employment replacing self-employment as the primary means of livelihood.

Yet, America continues to be associated the world over with the spirit of self-determination that embodies its roots as an entrepreneurial, self-reliant society. Furthermore, in economic downturns, job loss and lack of employment opportunities may produce additional incentive to pursue self-employment for people in a variety of situations and circumstances.

People with disabilities demonstrate the same passion, independence and self-direction as all Americans, and given certain characteristics—including being on average older and less educated—it is not surprising that the rate of self-employment for people with disabilities in the labor force in 2011 was about 50 percent higher than the corresponding rate for people without disabilities. In 2011, among employed individuals, a higher proportion of those with disabilities were unincorporated self-employed (11.8 percent) than individuals without disabilities (6.6 percent).[1]

2. Congress Establishes a National Initiative on Self-Employment for People with Disabilities

Congress provided $5,000,000 in the FY 2006 appropriation for the Department of Labor's (DOL) Office of Disability Employment Policy (ODEP) to develop research-based policy and provide technical assistance to organizations geared toward achieving sustainable self-employment outcomes for individuals with disabilities. (See Departments of Labor, Health and Human Services, Education and Related Agencies Appropriations Act, 2006, Public Law 109–149, Title I, 119 Stat. 2833, 2841 (2005); H.R. Conf. Rep. No. 109–300, at 59 (2005); S. Rep. No.109–103, at 26 (2005)). Previously, the Presidential Task Force on Employment of Adults with Disabilities (Executive Order 13078, 1998) had also encouraged self-employment. Furthermore, the Workforce Investment Act (WIA) and other federal programs that serve people with disabilities include self-employment as an outcome, but no prior federal initiative actively targeted self-employment as an outcome specifically for people with disabilities. The Senate Appropriations Committee Report provided the rationale for START-UP, stating:

> *The Committee is aware of the outstanding success of national non-profits working to increase self-employment among people with disabilities. Self-employment can provide income, assets and other elements of self-sufficiency to people with disabilities who are hard to place in traditional work environments, because of the flexibility inherent in self-employment. In addition to the direct benefit to the business owner, and the savings to the Social Security Disability Income (SSDI) program resulting from self-employment, preliminary data suggest that business owners with disabilities are far more likely to hire other people with disabilities as their businesses expand.*
>
> *Within the funds provided for ODEP, the Committee has included $5,000,000 for a national initiative focusing on self-employment as an option for people with disabilities. As the centerpiece of this new*

---

[1] http://www.bls.gov/news.release/disabl.t04.htm.

initiative, the Committee has included $3,000,000 to assist state job training institutions, WIA one stops, Small Business Administration (SBA) small business development centers, the vocational rehabilitation and employment services of the Department of Veterans Affairs (VA), state and tribal Vocational Rehabilitation (VR) agencies and other related programs in implementing effective and accessible practices for achieving sustainable self-employment outcomes for individuals with disabilities. Practices should include, but not be limited to, providing public education, training, technical assistance and accessible online and print resources with the purpose of advancing self-employment opportunities for Americans with disabilities. The Committee directs that, in making the national technical assistance grant, priority be given to national non-profits with experience in delivering direct consumer services, as well as training, to public and private agencies. The remainder of the funds in the initiative should be used to undertake a thorough analysis of the structures currently in place that either promote or impede the expansion of business ownership in the disability community.[2]

Based on this Congressional directive, START-UP was funded by ODEP in October 2006. Three separate START-UP demonstration cooperative agreement grants were awarded to consortia in Alaska, Florida, and New York, and one national-scale Self-Employment Technical Assistance, Resources and Training technical assistance center (START-UP/USA) cooperative agreement was awarded to a consortium headed by Virginia Commonwealth University (VCU). The goals of each of the three state consortia were to research, test, and evaluate innovative models of self-employment service delivery at the sub-national level to determine if those models could be adopted across the country. START-UP USA had four goals: 1) develop research-based policy, 2) provide technical assistance to the three state and local START-UP projects, 3) provide direct technical assistance to individual aspiring entrepreneurs from across the country to assist them to meet their self-employment goals, and 4) provide technical assistance to related systems that could implement practices for achieving sustainable self-employment outcomes for people with disabilities.

3. Self-Employment Among People with Disabilities

Self-employment allows people to customize their work experiences specifically to their needs and to design a work environment that optimizes flexibility and accommodation. Several public programs support employment preparation and work incentives to achieve self-sufficiency. Although limited, available statistics indicate that there has been little engagement by public programs to help people with disabilities explore self- employment as a viable work option. Prior to START-UP, several federal programs acknowledged self- employment as an outcome for people both with and without disabilities, but with few exceptions,[3] it is fair to say that not many programs specifically *promoted* self-employment.

The WIA, which authorizes DOL's American Job Centers (AJCs) (formerly known as One-Stop Career Centers), makes numerous references to self-employment. In fact, self-employment, entrepreneurship and small

---

[2] Senate Report Rep. No. 109–103, at 26 (2005).

[3] Project GATE (Growing America Through Entrepreneurship) was initiated in 2003 to help emerging entrepreneurships create, sustain and/or expand their existing small business. To help emerging entrepreneurs, Project GATE teamed ETA training and assistance programs with economic development entities, such as local Small Business Development Centers (SBDCs), women's business development centers, local chambers of commerce, entrepreneurial service providers and small business loan providers. The success of the original Project Gate led ETA to award four new Project GATE II grants in 2008 for the extension of the Project GATE model to federal dislocated workers in rural areas and over the age of 45. The evaluation, available at
http://wdr.doleta.gov/research/FullText_Documents/Findings%20from%20the%20Evaluation%20of%20Project%20GATE%20Report.pdf
found that Project GATE increased the probability of owning a business in the first few quarters after random assignment. Impacts were stronger for participants receiving unemployment insurance (UI) at the time of random assignment than for the full sample. In the 1990s, Congress authorized the Self-Employment Assistance (SEA) initiative which resulted in participants being 19 times more likely to be self-employed at any time after their spell of unemployment than nonparticipants. The evaluation report is available at
http://wdr.doleta.gov/research/keyword.cfm?fuseaction=dsp_puListingDetails&pub_id=2293&mp=y&start=121&sort=7.

businesses are mentioned in WIA, as amended, in several titles and sections: definitions; migrant and seasonal farm workers programs; demonstration, pilot, multi-service research, and multi-state projects; employment statistics; people with significant disabilities; VR services for individuals and groups; research; special projects and demonstrations; and provider and individual training. Furthermore, self-employment is an allowed exit outcome for individuals receiving services authorized by WIA. In 2010, the Employment and Training Administration (ETA) issued guidance on self-employment to state and local workforce agencies and rapid response coordinators.[4] But the proportion of AJC exiters who entered self-employment is unknown. AJCs report outcomes as employment of any type, with no distinction between self-employment and wage employment.

In 2011, ETA reported that 4.3 percent of all 2010 WIA exiters disclosed disabilities, and 3 percent who exited for employment reported disabilities.[5] ETA reported that less than 1 percent of WIA exiters in 2010 received entrepreneurial training,[6] suggesting that a very small percentage of all exiters (with and without disclosed disabilities) prepared for self-employment.

The Social Security Administration (SSA) sponsors work incentive programs to encourage employment of people with disabilities who receive Social Security Disability Insurance (SSDI) and Supplemental Security Income (SSI) due to disability. SSA's Plan to Achieve Self-Support (PASS)[7] and Ticket to Work[8] incentive programs include self-employment as an outcome for people with disabilities, but available data suggest self-employment is an infrequent outcome for program exiters.

ETA sponsored a study that matched AJC clients in four states (Colorado, Iowa, Maryland, and Oregon) with SSI and SSDI records to find out what proportion received SSA disability benefits (information not routinely recorded by AJCs). In Program Years 2002–2007, in all four states, only 2-4 percent of AJC users were SSA beneficiaries when they registered for services; slightly higher percentages (3 -6 percent) had once been SSA beneficiaries.[9] Despite these low percentages, AJCs served a substantial percentage of all SSA beneficiaries actively seeking employment (26 percent in Iowa and Colorado). These percentages are similar to, or much greater than, the percentage of SSA beneficiaries receiving employment services from vocational rehabilitation (VR) agencies in the same states.

People with disabilities may prepare for employment through their state VR programs, funded by the Rehabilitation Services Administration (RSA) in the Department of Education. RSA collects data on self-

---

[4] Training and Employment Guidance Letter 12-10, issued November 15, 2010. Available at http://wdr.doleta.gov/directives/attach/TEGL/TEGL12-10acc.pdf.

[5] U.S. Department of Labor, Employment and Training Administration. *PY 2010 Characteristics and Services of WIA Exiters with Positive and Negative Outcomes, Adult.* (Derived from PY 2010Q4 WIASRD Records) November 28, 2011. p.1. http://www.doleta.gov/Performance/results/Pdf/py10_adult_charact_services_positive_negative.pdf.

[6] U.S. Department of Labor, Employment and Training Administration. *PY 2010 Characteristics and Services of WIA Exiters with Positive and Negative Outcomes, Adult.* (Derived from PY 2010Q4 WIASRD Records) November 28, 2011. p.3. http://www.doleta.gov/Performance/results/Pdf/py10_adult_charact_services_positive_negative.pdf.

[7] Plans for Achieving Self-Support (PASS). The PASS provisions under the Social Security Act are an opportunity for individuals with disabilities to accumulate income and/or resources without causing either ineligibility for SSI or a reduction in benefit payments. Under an approved PASS, an individual may set aside earned income, unearned income and/or resources in a special account to pay for items or services needed to achieve a specified occupational goal. These income and/or resources are completely disregarded when determining an individual's eligibility for SSI or in calculating the SSI payment amount. Furthermore, federal regulations require that PASS funds be excluded by Medicaid, TANF, food stamps and HUD rental assistance programs. More information is available at http://www.idaresources.org/page?pageid=a047000000AsH85.

[8] The Ticket to Work Program provides most people receiving Social Security benefits (beneficiaries) more choices for receiving employment services. Under this program, most beneficiaries become eligible for the Ticket to Work Program when they start to receive SSDI or SSI benefits based on disability. Beneficiaries may choose to assign their tickets to an Employment Network (EN) of their choice to obtain employment services, vocational rehabilitation services or other support services necessary to achieve a vocational goal. The EN, if it accepts the ticket, will coordinate and provide appropriate services to help the beneficiary find and maintain employment. More information is available at http://www.chooseworkttw.net/about-program/faq.html.

[9] Livermore, Gina A. and Colman, Silvie. *Use of One Stops by Social Security Disability Beneficiaries in Four States Implementing Disability Program Navigator Initiatives: Final Report.* May 2010. p. xi.

employment outcomes for people with disabilities who receive VR services. The Rehabilitation Act of 1973, Sections 7(11) (C) and 103(a) (13), supports state VR agencies in offering a self-employment outcome as follows:

(C) Satisfying any other vocational outcome the Secretary may determine to be appropriate (including satisfying the vocational outcome of self-employment, telecommuting or business ownership), in a manner consistent with the Act.

(13) Technical assistance and other consultation services to conduct market analyses, develop business plans, and otherwise provide resources, to the extent such resources are authorized to be provided through the statewide workforce investment system, to eligible individuals who are pursuing self-employment or telecommuting or establishing a small business operation as an employment outcome.

Despite this authority, an analysis of RSA case closure statistics for VR clients indicated that self-employment remains a small percentage of overall VR status 26 closures in employment, ranging from 1.97 percent in 2003 to 1.66 percent in 2007 and 1.99 percent in 2009, although there has been a small increase to 2.40 percent in 2012.[10]

VR agencies with the highest percentage of self-employment outcomes were in states generally considered to have more disbursed populations and generally more rural communities.

Average hourly and weekly earnings for individuals closed in self-employment were consistently higher than the average wages for all Status 26 (successfully employed) closures. The average hourly wage for persons closed in self-employment in FY 2012 was $14.46, compared to $11.33 for all Status 26 closures. Average weekly wage in self-employment in FY 2012 was $445, compared to $365 for all Status 26 closures.

The mean average case service expenditure by VR agencies for persons closed in self-employment in FY 2012 was approximately $7,910. In comparison, the average expenditure for all Status 26 closures in FY 2012 was approximately $5,436.

The mean average time period from the point that the Individual Plan for Employment was initiated to closure in self-employment in FY 2012 was 663 days. The comparative time period for all Status 26 closures in employment was 630 days.

VR State agency involvement in facilitating self-employment outcomes does vary substantially from state to state, particularly for persons with a primary intellectual disability. There are states, such as Florida and Ohio, whose VR agencies are involved in initiatives to implement policies and practices that expand participation in self-employment. These agencies are implementing a step-by-step vocational rehabilitation process that provides a variety of resources to the individual with a disability potentially interested in self-employment. This process focuses on individual support needs and emphasizes the development of a business design team to assist and support the self-employment initiative. It also focuses on the ongoing supports needed for the development of a viable business plan and the successful implementation and maintenance of the self-employment venture.

---

[10] West, Michael D. *Access to Public Self-Employment Opportunities and Resources for Individuals with Disabilities.* Virginia Commonwealth University, December 2008. RSA case closure statistics are currently available for each state, not nationally. VCU analyzed the national data as part of the START-UP/USA grant. 2012 data provided by RSA based on 2012 RSA-911 report data.

2. KEY ELEMENTS OF THE ODEP START-UP GRANTS

One National Technical Assistance Center and Three State Grantees

In 2011, ODEP funded Economic Systems Inc. to examine key elements, outcomes and impacts, and successes of the START-UP grants, as well as identify policy and systems barriers and propose recommendations for the future. This analysis, contained in the following pages, derived from two main sources: 1) existing reports and websites produced by the four START-UP grantees, and 2) interviews with the leadership of the four START-UP grantees. In-person interviews were conducted in Syracuse for START-UP /New York. The leadership of START-UP/Alaska, START-UP/Florida, and START-UP/USA were interviewed by phone. The interviews and site visit were completed in January and February of 2012.

START-UP/USA and all three state initiatives used a non-traditional assessment process, referred to as "discovery," which is the foundation of the innovative strategy of Customized Employment. The traditional model of employment services consists of determining employer needs and then finding a person with a disability to fulfill those needs. Customized employment, in contrast, considers an individual's talents and desires first, and the business idea follows. Thus, "discovery" in the context of self-employment is the customized approach to assisting an individual with a disability in pursuing entrepreneurship. Typically, discovery begins with conversations with the individual and family members, friends, and other acquaintances to learn about the individual's interests, talents, and needed support strategies. These discussions, plus observations in the home, neighborhood, and workplace, if appropriate, reveal existing social capital, business expertise, connections, and experiences, which may be helpful if the individual launches an enterprise.

The discovery process seeks to reveal personal themes that can be used to develop goals for employment. Questions addressed during the discovery process include, but are not limited to, the following:

- When is this person at his or her best?
- What support strategies are needed in particular situations?
- How does the individual learn best?
- Who knows the individual well?
- What circumstances may make the individual anxious or frightened?
- When is the person "in flow" (i.e., at peak performance or most comfortable)?[11]

Discovery guided START-UP candidates in analyzing whether self-employment was appropriate and feasible for them to pursue. Some candidates did not pursue self-employment because of either failing to pursue discovery or concluding that self-employment was not their best employment option.

1. The START-UP National Technical Assistance Center (START-UP/USA)

The national technical assistance center, START-UP/USA, was developed by VCU's Rehabilitation Research Training Center on Workplace Supports (VCU-RRTC) in collaboration with Griffin-Hammis Associates, LLC. Its work fell under four main tasks:

1. Provided direct technical assistance to the three state grantees, based on the identified needs of each project, and offered support tailored to meet those needs.

2. Developed a technical assistance center designed to increase the capacity of existing systems to provide self-employment services to people with disabilities. This center included a Web site, www.start-up-usa.biz

---

[11] Griffin, Cary. *Discovery*. http://www.start-up-usa.biz/resources/content.cfm?id=696.

with online resources, materials and links; a webinar series on topics of interest; and online courses.

3. Provided technical assistance to individual potential entrepreneurs through mail, phone and email support.

4. Conducted nationwide research and analysis of current resources and support available to individuals with disabilities for pursuit of entrepreneurship.

2. The Three State Grants

Each of the three START-UP state demonstration grantees in Alaska, Florida, and New York developed its own collaborative model involving key stakeholders. These stakeholders represented advocacy; small business development; university programs; and rehabilitative, training and employment services for people with disabilities. Each of the three state demonstration sites also established a collaborative work group, developed and implemented training programs for front-line staff, and provided direct services to people with disabilities who were interested in pursuing self-employment. The general approach used by all three state grantees can be summarized as follows:

- Established a consortium to develop the program, typically involving:
  - State's department of labor (associated with U.S. Department of Labor)
  - State's VR agency (associated with U.S. Department of Education)
  - Small business development centers (SBDCs) (Associated with U.S. Small Business Administration)
  - Advocacy groups
  - Universities
- Developed, trained and implemented a curriculum for counselors and people with disabilities in:
  - Discovery assessment process for self-employment readiness
  - Support in developing a business plan
  - Support in obtaining financing
  - Support in carrying out the business plan
- Provided direct assistance to people with disabilities

3. START-UP Initiative in Alaska (START-UP/Alaska)

Purpose

START-UP/Alaska intended to build on the state's prior efforts to develop a customized employment[12] self-employment program and to develop the infrastructure needed to overcome barriers to self-employment for people with disabilities. The Governor's Council on Disability and Self-Employment led the Alaska consortia, beginning with 10 stakeholders, including the state's VR agency, AJCs, and SBDCs. The consortium met to identify needs, map resources, and identify infrastructure issues that needed to be remedied. The customized self-employment model was implemented at three sites, including two AJCs and one independent living center that worked closely with the nearby AJC. A Virtual Business Advisor was also used to assist potential entrepreneurs in remote areas of the state in developing a formal business plan and to provide ongoing support until their businesses were self-sufficient.

---

[12] From 2001 to 2006, ODEP funded 20 demonstration projects, including Alaska, to provide customized employment through AJCs, as well as non-profit and faith-based agencies. Customized employment is an employment strategy that matches the specific skills, interests and needs of the job seeker with the unmet workplace needs of the employer through a newly customized position or to become self-employed. It is based on an individualized determination of the strengths, requirements and interests of a person and an assessment of the organizational and operational needs of a particular employer. Additional information on customized employment is available at http://www.dol.gov/odep/categories/workforce/CustomizedEmployment/what/index.htm .

Scale

START-UP/Alaska covered the cities of Anchorage, Juneau, and Fairbanks and their surrounding areas. The Juneau site expanded to cover southeast Alaska through virtual services.

Target Populations

Clients accessed START-UP/Alaska services through a variety of referral sources, such as Division of Vocational Rehabilitation (DVR) counselors, Disability Program Navigators (DPN) based at AJCs, colleagues, SBDCs, school districts, Client Assistance Programs (CAPs), and self-referrals. START-UP/Alaska characterized some of the referrals as individuals for whom counselors had already "tried everything," yet had not succeeded in achieving wage employment. Candidates went through a formal "discovery" process, conceptualized by Marc Gold and Associates and offered through Employment for All, an offshoot of Marc Gold and Associates, as well as through Griffin-Hammis Associates, LLC, a member of the START-UP/USA consortium.

START-UP/Alaska planned to provide services to 10 people with significant disabilities in each of the 3 locations, or help a total of 30 people with significant disabilities become self-employed as a result of the interventions of the demonstration. Actually, 78 individuals received services, 37 completed a business plan and 33 created businesses.

Critical Elements of Alaska Model

START-UP/Alaska used a business incubator model with customized self-employment, supported by resources provided by START-UP/USA and three self-employment facilitators with business start-up expertise. All START-UP/Alaska candidates who chose to pursue self-employment went through a discovery process as the first step toward developing a customized self-employment business. Initially planned as a physical incubator in a single location, the rural nature and size of the coverage area led to the implementation of the virtual incubator model. The approach successfully used electronic tools to provide entrepreneurs and site facilitators with business development, management training and technical assistance, including Internet-based webinars, teleconferences, and one-on-one phone calls.

4. START-UP Initiative in Florida (START-UP/Florida)

Purpose

Florida's Agency for Workforce Innovation (AWI) led a consortium of stakeholders in developing a strategy for supporting self-employment for Floridians with disabilities. The goals identified by the START-UP/Florida state-level steering committee were to: 1) increase economic self-sufficiency and personal independence of individuals with disabilities by taking full advantage of financial supports, program waivers and other incentives available at the federal, state and local levels; 2) increase opportunities for people with disabilities to become self-employed or become entrepreneurs by creating their own microenterprises; and 3) increase the assets and economic self-sufficiency of individuals and targeted communities.

Scale

Jacksonville (targeted veterans with disabilities), Lakeland (targeted people with developmental disabilities), and Ft. Lauderdale/Miami (targeted all people with disabilities) were selected for intensive training and technical assistance. They then served as incubators for further expansion of the models tested through START-UP/Florida.

Target Populations

START-UP/Florida targeted youth, adults, veterans, and older workers with disabilities.

Critical Elements of Florida Model

START-UP/Florida tested three models that had been previously developed and used in Florida to build capacity and infrastructure for people with disabilities interested in self-employment. The START-UP/Florida grant was designed to study the impact of and build upon these three models at both the systems and individual levels. Thus, collaborative partners included the agencies involved with the three models: the state's workforce innovation agency, VR agency and Department of Education; the University of South Florida; and the Association for Persons with Developmental Disabilities. AJCs were used as the primary training location in several sites.

The three models implemented and tested were METTA (Micro-Enterprise Training and Technical Assistance), BOSS (Bridging Opportunities for Self-Sufficiency) and FastTrac (a private-sector self-employment training curriculum). Developed by the University of South Florida, the METTA model is highly interactive, with a defined discovery process and team approach that integrates partners across disciplines working toward the goal of self-employment for individuals who are mostly VR-eligible with significant disabilities. The model's training includes professional and technical assistance curricula for people located in both urban and rural communities.

Developed by Florida's Department of Education, the BOSS model is essentially a manual designed for educators and human services' professionals to help individuals with disabilities explore and pursue the option of self-employment as a career choice. The model consists of a four-step process: 1) identification of a primary support person; 2) selection of the support team; 3) exploration and examination of relevant information about the individual's life, dreams, talents, supports and relationships; and 4) development of the BOSS Self-Folio. The BOSS model is an action-oriented tool that has been used to assist students in transition from high school to work. START-UP/Florida also used BOSS in conjunction with METTA as a tool for individuals transitioning from school to work, as well as for others already out of school.

A nationally recognized entrepreneurial training program that has a developed curriculum, FastTrac uses certified facilitators and materials to provide entrepreneurial training. FastTrac was introduced by AWI in AJCs prior to START-UP/Florida as a viable self-employment training option for veterans with disabilities.

5. START-UP Initiative in New York (START-UP/New York)

Purpose

The Burton Blatt Institute (BBI) at Syracuse University led START-UP/New York, the goal of which was to establish a sustainable public-private sector collaboration that provides all necessary supports to offer people with diverse disabilities effective and meaningful opportunities to pursue and obtain self-employment.

Scale

START-UP/New York was conducted in Onondaga County, in which Syracuse is the largest city. By the end of the grant period, START-UP/New York had also begun to establish programs in surrounding counties and New York City.

Target Populations

START-UP/New York sought referrals in Onondaga County through direct advertising, partner agencies and the state public workforce system. Individuals with disabilities were recruited inclusively by START-UP/New York, without regard for the nature or severity of their disability. Interested persons with disabilities went through a discovery process in which they explored their interests, strengths and support systems. Individuals who concluded that they wanted to pursue entrepreneurship at the end of their discovery experience continued into ongoing support from START-UP/New York.

Critical Elements of New York Model

The START-UP/New York program was built and delivered using a strong network of multi-stakeholder partners and collaborators. In addition to the BBI, these key stakeholders included Syracuse University's Institute for Veterans and Military Families and Whitman School of Management; the county VR agency; the South Side Innovation Center (SSIC) small business incubator; and the local SBDC. By June 2009, START-UP/New York had engaged 55 stakeholders, including the program management team; research universities and colleges; financial institutions; disability service agencies at the county, state and national levels; and technology and economic development agencies.

START-UP/New York's model used a business incubator operated at the SSIC in Syracuse to support entrepreneurs through the discovery process and ongoing peer-to-peer networking meetings during which participants shared experiences. Prospective entrepreneurs first met with an SSIC staff member designated as a "Business Navigator." After discovery, the SSIC connected the entrepreneurs with the state's VR agency and SBDC, which provided advice and business training needed for a successful business launch. The Business Navigator and SBDC staff then continued to follow and advise entrepreneurs following launch to ensure sustainability of the business.

As the project evolved, START-UP/New York developed a graduate and undergraduate course, entitled *Inclusive Entrepreneurship,* offered through Syracuse University's Whitman School of Management. The course familiarizes management majors with the issues that people with disabilities face when they seek entrepreneurship. Students enrolled in the course are assigned to consulting teams to work with START-UP/New York entrepreneurs in developing their business plans and marketing materials, identifying financing, and conducting related activities.

START-UP/New York's BBI team also worked closely with the Whitman School-led Entrepreneurship Bootcamp for Veterans (EBV) program started in 2007 to develop a customized program for veterans with disabilities. This program provides cutting edge, experiential training in entrepreneurship and small business management to post-9/11 veterans with disabilities and is offered entirely free to qualified candidates accepted into the program. BBI is a collaborative EBV partner for creating disability-related curriculum and assisting participants in understanding and leveraging programs at the intersection of disability and entrepreneurship. The EBV program is currently offered by a network of six world-class institutions.

3. OUTCOMES AND IMPACTS

1. The Context for START-UP Self-Employment Outcomes

State START-UP grantees consistently reported that the workforce development system and state VR agencies are not oriented toward entrepreneurship and self-employment as employment outcomes for people with disabilities. Instead, these programs and services emphasize wage employment, as shown below in Figure 1.

Figure 1: General Path to Employment for People with a Disability

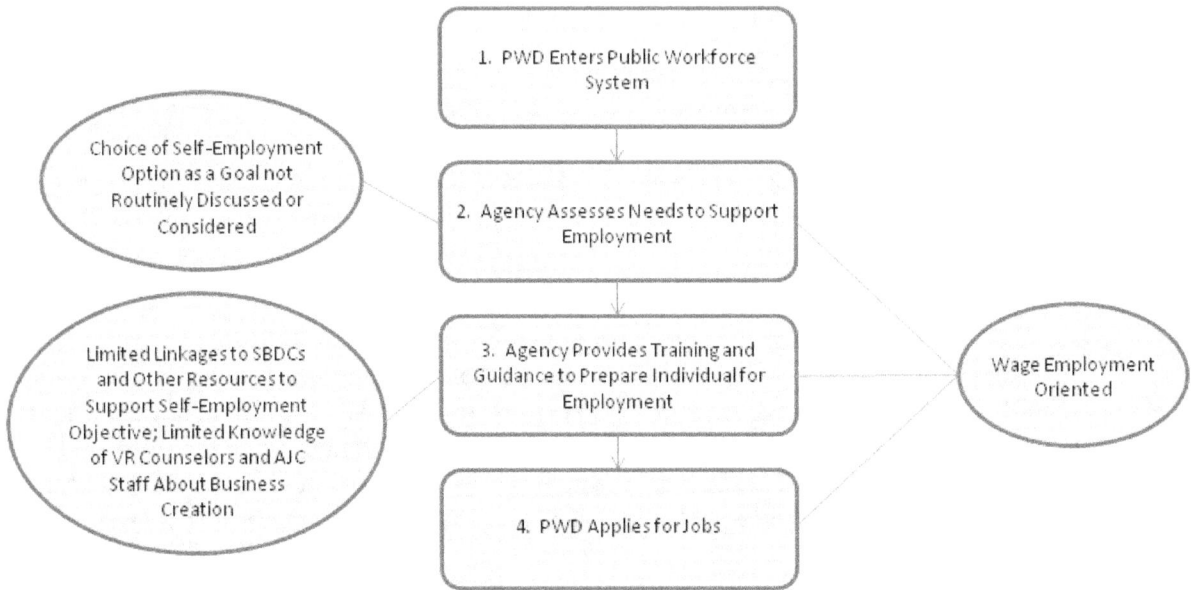

For people with disabilities interested in pursuing self-employment, the path requires substantial initiative, tenacity and skills, just as it does for people without disabilities. Agencies are generally oriented to supporting individuals in seeking wage employment and thus are better prepared to support that path. Figure 2 illustrates the path a person with a disability might follow in the public workforce system, with linkages to other sources of support.

Figure 2: General Path for People with Disabilities Seeking Self-Employment

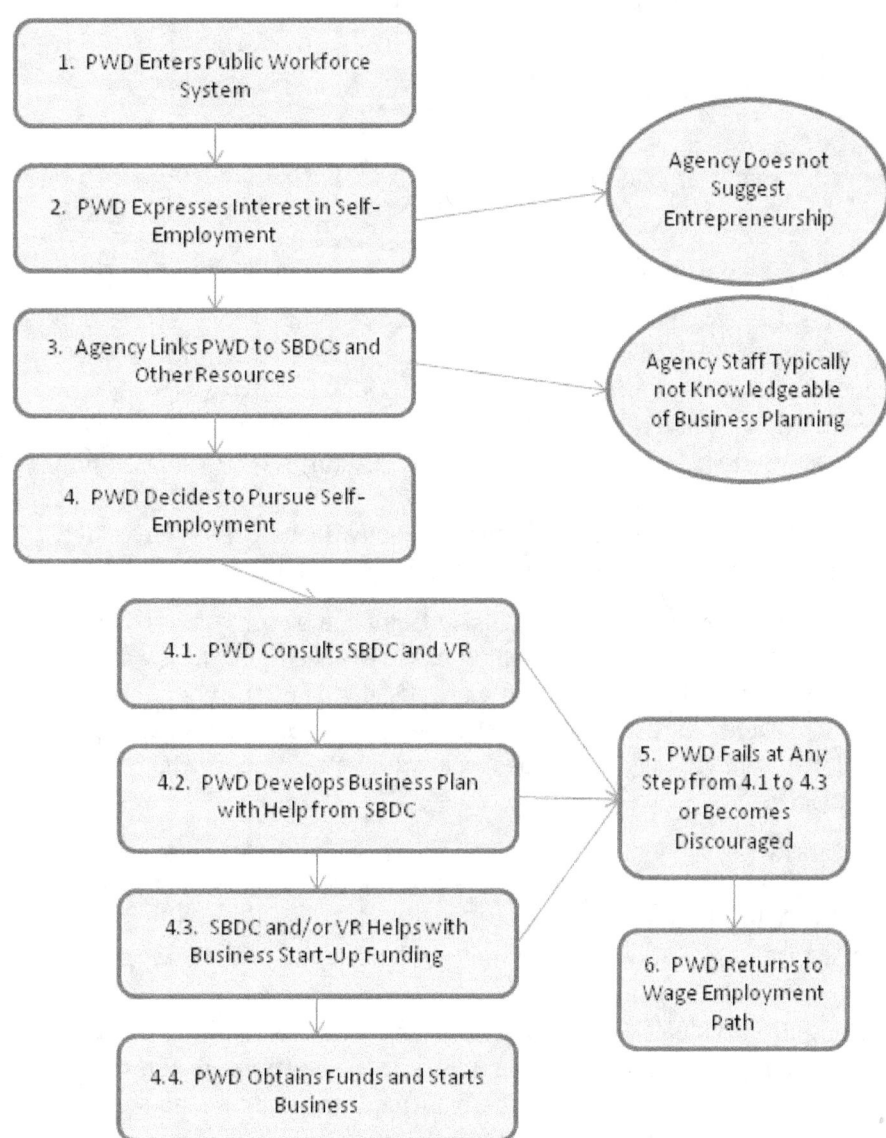

The three demonstration sites reported that prior to START-UP, self-employment was not a typical outcome for a person with a disability seeking assistance from the state's VR agency or an AJC. VCU analyzed the RSA 911 data system (performance data RSA collects annually from state VR programs) and found that nationally, VR agencies produced a 1.99 percent rate of self-employment among the cases they closed in 2009.

State grantees met the following perceived barriers, to varying degrees:

- A culture that was not oriented toward self-employment for people with disabilities. Staff involved with START-UP reported that some stakeholders held the belief that self-employment is not viable or feasible for most people with disabilities.

- Unrealistic expectations for business plan development. Some staff involved with START-UP reported that some stakeholders had expectations for people with no prior business experience to develop business plans independently and without much support.

- Lack of infrastructure to support self-employment, including absence of communication and coordination among organizations involved in supporting people with disabilities in seeking self-employment.

- Lack of understanding among front-line staff about entrepreneurship and the tools and resources needed to support self-employment among people with disabilities.

- Federal Social Security disability benefit policies that create disincentives to employment overall[13] and federal workforce system program policies[14] that discourage choice and pursuit of self-employment.

- Performance measures for AJCs that are wage-driven do not consider business start-up as a relevant indicator of success.

- Lack of financial resources and access to capital for entrepreneurs to support business start-up.

VCU interviewed 23 successful (defined as having been in business at least 12 months and having achieved $10,000 in revenue) entrepreneurs with disabilities about their experiences in getting support for self-employment from existing systems prior to START-UP. Interview participants indicated that their core case coordination contact points were *not* a primary source for assistance in pursuing self-employment. Local mental health case management and treatment systems, secondary-level public education programs, and community rehabilitation programs and employment services organizations generally did not proactively offer information on self-employment options during vocational assessment and career exploration activities. In general, staff members of these programs were generally not knowledgeable about self-employment.

Rather, the entrepreneurs with disabilities interviewed said a significant factor in their success was finding an individual who could champion and facilitate an exploration of self-employment. Such individuals were found in community non-profit programs or a unit of a public program that had a specific focus on entrepreneurship. Self-employment champions, programs and agencies are occasionally available, but not widely, to support people with disabilities. VCU also observed that state VR programs tended to support entrepreneurs who had obtained multiple funding sources for their business.[15]

The situation for a person with a disability was significantly different in the state START-UP demonstrations. These demonstrations brought together existing resources to support self-employment and used START-UP resources to train agency staff and create an infrastructure to support people with disabilities in developing self-employment plans and goals for themselves. START-UP shifted the paradigm from one that assumed people with disabilities should pursue wage employment to one in which people with disabilities were encouraged to pursue self-employment. START-UP helped to inspire individuals with disabilities to consider self-employment. Most importantly, it overcame the systemic barriers that people with disabilities face when trying to pursue entrepreneurship. Figure 3 illustrates how the general path to self-employment and entrepreneurship changed for people with disabilities, following the approaches demonstrated by START-UP.

---

[13] Perceived disincentives are not expecting people to pursue employment after having been deemed "unemployable," potential loss of benefits due to employment income, and fear of not being able to get disability benefits again if self-employment does not work out.

[14] Program policies that discourage choice and self-employment are policies that encourage agencies to place people in employment as soon as possible and policies that do not have separate indicators for success for self-employment and wage employment. Self-employment typically takes more time to develop than wage employment.

[15] Virginia Commonwealth University. *START-UP/USA Final Close-Out Report*. December 10, 2010.

Figure 3: General Path for People with Disabilities Seeking Self-Employment after START-UP

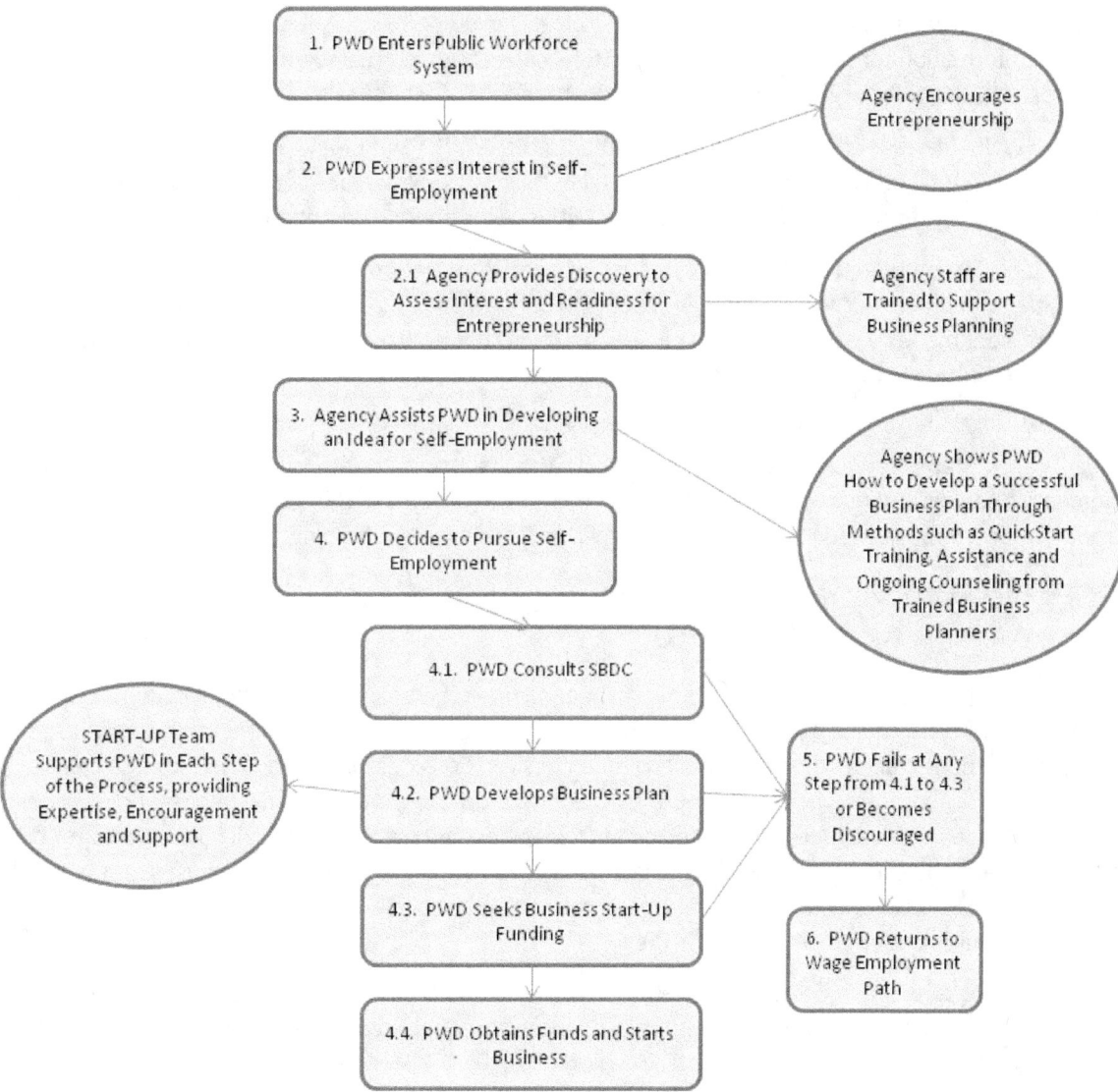

2. START-UP Accomplishments

VCU was responsible for collecting outcome data from all START-UP grantees, including START-UP/USA. START-UP accomplishments are presented in three categories: technical assistance, capacity-building, and numbers of participants. Except as otherwise noted, all quantitative information on accomplishments are those reported in VCU's close-out report cited previously.

a. Technical Assistance

VCU's START-UP/USA reported the following accomplishments for the START-UP/USA website and technical assistance center during START-UP's funding period:

- From January 1, 2007 through December 10, 2010, a total of 73,922 visitors came to the START-UP/USA website. A total of 270,218 page views were made by these visitors.

- START-UP/USA produced and streamed 19 live webcasts. A total of 2,613 individuals participated in the webcasts during the course of the project. (See Appendix 1 for a list of the webcasts topics.)

- Webcasts were made available through online archives, which were used by 11,276 visitors with a total of 17,442 page views through December 10, 2010.

- VCU developed and acquired resources for the website, including 18 fact sheets, 8 case studies, and links to relevant information for business start-up. The 18 fact sheets were accessed by 12,866 individuals during the project with a total of 28,576 page views. (See Appendix 2 for a list of fact sheets.)

- START-UP/USA developed an online course entitled "Overview of Self-Employment for Entrepreneurs with Disabilities." A total of 335 individuals participated in the course between April 2009 and November 2010. The course is still offered regularly as of the date of this publication. (See Appendix 3 for more information.)

- START-UP/USA completed 1,422 technical assistance and information requests made by people with disabilities and others between October 1, 2007 and September 30, 2010. Almost half (46.1 percent) of the requests were made by people with disabilities and their families. The next largest group of requests came from community rehabilitation providers, at 17.6 percent. Requests were completed by email, web, phone, and in-person.

- Technical assistance requests were most frequently about starting a business (38.3 percent), funding (30.1 percent), and policies and supports (19.1 percent). About two-thirds of the technical assistance requests about funding were related to work incentives, waivers, and blended funding.

b. Capacity-Building

Systems Change

The three state grantees were engaged in systems change. All project managers interviewed in January and February of 2012 reported increased capacity and coordination through the development of new collaborations and relationships among stakeholders and breaking down of silos. Considerable effort went into building trust and consensus among collaborators whose goals were focused more on wage employment than self-employment for people with disabilities. Stakeholders signed memoranda of understanding, defining their roles and common goals. Meetings, team-building activities, and retreats were used by the grantees to build consensus on the idea of entrepreneurship for people with disabilities. Not all consortia members were convinced initially that self-employment was feasible for people with disabilities.

Each START-UP state consortium coordinated resources from the public and private sectors, including government, higher education, non-profit community agencies, for-profit companies, and advocacy groups. Figure 4 presents the collaborators in each state.

Once an appropriate level of consensus was achieved, START-UP consortia worked to become knowledgeable in the multiple facets of supporting self-employment for people with disabilities. The facets included consultation in business planning, marketing, advertising, financing, licensure, and numerous other aspects specific to the nature of a particular business. This knowledge was then used to provide customized services to people with disabilities.

Leveraging Funding

A critical concern to all state demonstration sites was raising funds for business start-up while maintaining support through disability benefits from Social Security, maintaining health care from Medicaid, and channeling work-incentive funding to support START-UP businesses. Grantees that were most successful in addressing funding issues for their entrepreneurs obtained financing from foundations and non-profits. All grantees worked closely with START-UP/USA on strategies to leverage funds from work-incentive programs and to prevent entrepreneurs from losing their benefits during the critical phase of launching their businesses.

Figure 4: Collaborators in START-UP States

START UP/Alaska	START UP/Florida	START UP/New York
Governor's Council on Disabilities and Special Education	Workforce Florida, Inc.	Burton Blatt Institute at Syracuse University
Alaska Division of Vocational Rehabilitation	Agency for Persons with Disabilities	South Side Entrepreneurial Connect Project and Incubator of the Walt Whitman School of Business at Syracuse University
Alaska Employment Security Division	Florida Division of Vocational Rehabilitation	Institute for Veterans and Military Families
Alaska Division of Business Partnerships	Three Florida Regional Workforce Boards	ARISE Independent Living Center
Alaska Division of Public Assistance	University of South Florida	Advocates for Living Potential
Alaska Division of Behavioral Health	Griffin-Hammis LLC	CNY Works
Alaska Division of Senior and Disability Services	National Disability Institute	Enable
Alaska Division of Teaching and Learning Support		Greater Syracuse Chamber of Commerce
University of Alaska		Syracuse Cooperative Federal Credit Union
Small Business Development Center		Onondaga County Office of Economic Development
Alaska Mental Health Trust Authority		Office of Vocational and Educational Services for Individuals with Disabilities, New York State Education Department
Employment for All (EFA)		

PASS, for instance, is utilized by less than 1 percent of those eligible overall.[16] In contrast, one fourth (43 of 194 START-UP participants surveyed by VCU)[17] had PASS plans. START-UP/USA demonstrated how to use this resource by helping craft numerous PASS scenarios with business owners in the three states. With assistance from START-UP/USA, demonstration grantees leveraged PASS, VR funding, PESS[18] and Medicaid waiver funds for support of business development.[19] START-UP demonstration managers interviewed in 2012 reported that blending funds from these sources is a cumbersome and time-consuming process that requires specialized expertise. Although SSA counselors in the Work Incentive Planning and Assistance (WIPA) program were available and were consulted by grantees, there was still a need for grantees to provide additional benefits counseling to

---

[16] The Social Security Administration reported that 0.1 percent of SSI recipients who are blind or have other disabilities and worked in 2010 had a Plan to Achieve Self Sufficiency (PASS). http://www.ssa.gov/policy/docs/statcomps/ssi_asr/2010/ssi_asr10.pdf .

[17] Virginia Commonwealth University. *START-UP/USA Final Close-Out Report*. December 2010.

[18] Property Essential for Self Support. SSI allows unlimited accumulation of assets (including cash in a business account) for the operation of certain small businesses or micro-enterprises. PESS is excluded from Medicaid eligibility determinations, thereby allowing Medicaid to continue for business owners who received SSI disability benefits. See: http://www.socialsecurity.gov/redbook/eng/ssi-only-employment-supports.htm#4.

[19] Virginia Commonwealth University, *START-UP/USA Final Close-Out Report*. December 2010.

START-UP entrepreneurs. With assistance from START-UP/USA, START-UP demonstration grantees trained specialized benefits navigators to assist entrepreneurs.

Sustained Collaborations and Partnerships

In addressing barriers to self-employment, state grantees made formal and informal agreements, executed memoranda of understanding, developed manuals, wrote policy, instituted trainings for staff and for entrepreneurs, and uncovered features of existing programs and systems that supported and hindered self-employment for people with disabilities. For example, START-UP/Alaska developed memoranda of understanding between major stakeholders in the state to align policies in support of self-employment among people with disabilities. In Florida, the VR program revised its self-employment policy and funded staff development. Alaska's Division of Senior and Disability Services put in state Medicaid waiver regulations provisions to increase the service period so that longer-term support to nascent entrepreneurs could be provided and the businesses could be sustained. The New York State Senate introduced legislation in 2012, aimed at dramatically expanding entrepreneurship opportunities for veterans with disabilities. The bill, which was pending when this report went to press, referenced the work of the BBI at Syracuse University and reflected the success of START-UP/New York and the university course entitled Inclusive Entrepreneurship.

Curricula and Training

START-UP/Florida created a self-employment certification for its vendor network. By the end of 2010, more than 100 vendors had received certification in self-employment. START-UP/Florida also incorporated the BOSS self-employment manual into their high school curricula statewide to assist youth in transition.

As mentioned above, in New York, BBI and the Whitman School of Management at Syracuse University developed a course offered by the Whitman School to undergraduate and graduate business majors entitled Inclusive Entrepreneurship. The course sensitizes students to the issues faced by people with disabilities in employment and in self-employment, and students provide technical assistance to START-UP entrepreneurs.

VCU's START-UP/USA, in association with Griffin-Hammis Associates, LLC, refined approaches to discovery (assessment), marketing (the MicroMarketing materials), and business planning (the Quick-Launch Parts I and II Business Plan curriculum). They also provided extensive training and materials on SSA and U.S. Department of Veterans Affairs (VA) benefits relating to self-employment income and activities. State grantees received technical assistance and training in these approaches and adapted or implemented them in developing their own projects. All of the state grantees received training and technical assistance in implementing the discovery assessment process, during which START-UP candidates were coached to assess their desire and capacity to be an entrepreneur. START-UP/USA also provided training to staff and directly assisted entrepreneurs in planning and launching their businesses.

The Quick-Launch training curriculum was expanded by START-UP/USA. (See Figure 5.) Part I of Quick-Launch brought prospective business owners and their team members (START-UP state staff) together and led them step-by-step through the small business-planning map resulting in a draft business plan. The two-day Part I sessions gathered information from discovery, the rationale for a business instead of wage employment, the business model, a sales plan, pro-forma cash flow projections, a start-up budget, supplies, tools and equipment needed, the existence of competitors, marketing and distribution approaches, etc.

Part II of Quick-Launch pulled together the work between the initial planning and the addition of SSA work incentives, analyses of the impact of earnings on medical benefits, leveraging opportunities for financial and business supports, and the incorporation of feasibility testing into a useable business plan. While Quick-Launch was a training series, much of the actual writing and research took place leading up to and following the class sessions. This resulted in ongoing technical assistance to the prospective business owner, the team, family members offering support, and the various funders. This technical assistance effort demonstrated the intensity and the rigor of the process, and is now being used in numerous states across the country.

Figure 5: Small Business START-UP Flow Chart Used by the START-UP/USA in Quick-Launch Training

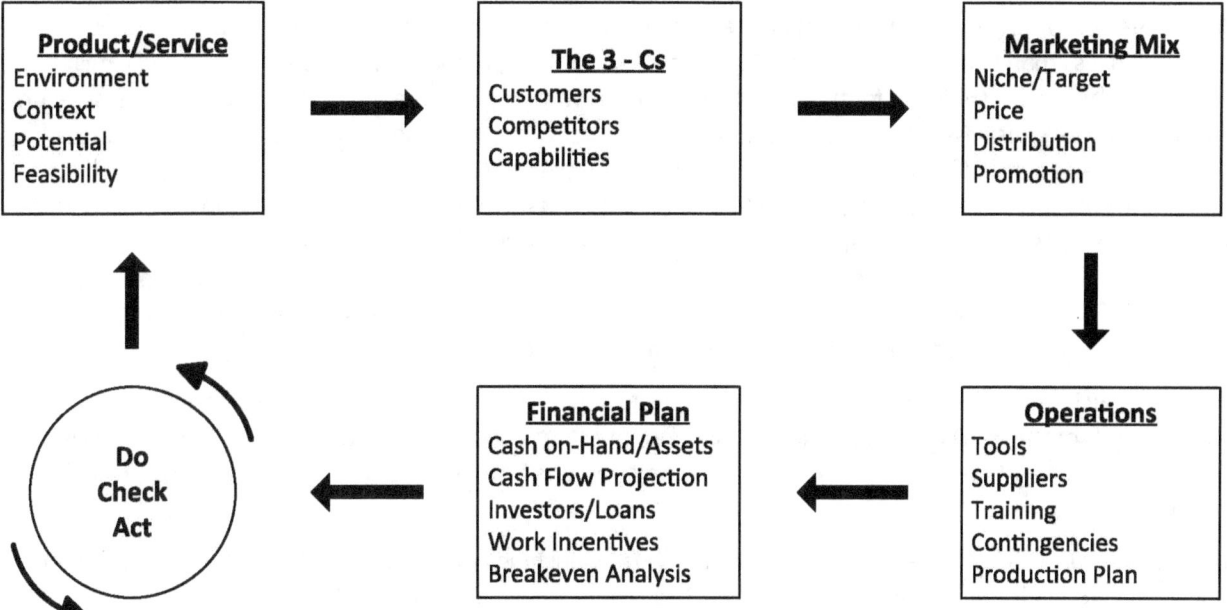

Source: Virginia Commonwealth University START-UP/USA Final Close-Out Report

Infrastructure

State grantees' goals included policy changes and infrastructure development, as well as entrepreneurship outcomes for people with disabilities enrolled in their programs. The level of infrastructure development and capacity to serve entrepreneurs with disabilities varied in the grantee sites. The Florida grantee leadership reported that prior to START-UP, little capacity existed to support entrepreneurship, and therefore it had to place more emphasis on planning, design, and development than actual service delivery. Other state grantees built upon existing systems. Alaska leadership, for instance, noted that self-employment was a natural offshoot to their customized employment grant (previously funded by ODEP). New York's BBI Institute built on its extensive experience in supporting wage employment of individuals with disabilities. With backing from the chancellor to improve the lives of people in the community, BBI marshaled stakeholders to support entrepreneurship among people with disabilities in Onondaga County, NY.

c. Number of Entrepreneurs

Given their different starting positions, the state grantees varied in their expectations for the third type of accomplishment: the number of entrepreneurs they anticipated would complete their programs. Alaska anticipated that it would produce about 7 or 8 entrepreneurs per local site, or a total of 30; Florida expected one successful entrepreneur per model, or a total of 3, and New York expected 30 entrepreneurs with disabilities would start businesses. START-UP/USA established a data reporting system for the state grantees to record information about the people with disabilities enrolled in their START-UP programs. During the period during which START-UP/USA collected data, all state grantees exceeded their expectations. Candidates for START-UP were recruited by referrals from stakeholder agencies, word of mouth, publicity about the projects and, in New York, direct outreach in the community. VCU recorded 194[20] people enrolled in START-UP services in the three participating states.[21]

---

[20] Although START-UP had 194 recorded participants, not all 194 provided data for each item in the reporting system. Findings are from respondents who provided data on the topic discussed, which could be fewer than all participants.

[21] Virginia Commonwealth University, *START-UP/USA Final Close-Out Report*, December 10, 2010.

3. Outcomes for Entrepreneurs

With grantees devoting the first year of their grants to planning and development, START-UP entrepreneurs typically had less than two years to launch a business and become operational. Available research indicates that less than two years is insufficient for nascent entrepreneurs, with or without a disability, to develop plans, secure financing, launch a business, and become established. The first U.S. Panel Study of Entrepreneurial Dynamics[22] (PSED) surveyed a panel of nascent entrepreneurs and found that after about four and a half years, about one-third of entrepreneurs were operating a new business, one-third were still in the active start-up phase, and one-third had disengaged from the entrepreneurial process.[23] ETA's Project GATE reported that it took an average of about a year[24] of support before their participants launched a business (Project GATE did not target people with disabilities). The two-year implementation was too short to expect many START-UP entrepreneurs to have entered the operational stage, yet with support from the grantees, many did.

Likewise, START-UP's implementation period was too short to expect businesses to generate an income and profit. Analysis of the PSED found that the median amount of time between the first organizing activity performed to start a business and the first receipt of money, income, or fees from the sale of goods and services was 25 months.

START-UP entrepreneurs exceeded many of the norms for launching new businesses. Of the 194 persons with disabilities enrolled in START-UP programming, 137 achieved at least one major milestone.[25] The most frequently achieved milestone was initiation of a business plan. During the period VCU gathered data, 56 entrepreneurs reported an operating business. A business could be defined as viable on the basis of having filed federal and state tax returns. Of the persons with disabilities supported by START-UP in the 3 states, 11 entrepreneurs in Alaska, 3 entrepreneurs in Florida and 23 entrepreneurs in New York filed federal tax returns.[26]

In the 2012 interviews, START-UP/Florida and START-UP/New York leadership said that more individuals pursued entrepreneurship than what was captured by the START-UP/USA reporting. START-UP/Florida leadership stated that the FastTrac model was implemented with veterans before the reporting system was established; therefore, the veteran entrepreneurs were not counted. START-UP/New York leadership reported a lengthy planning and development process, with far more individuals than reported to VCU in the pipeline. START-UP/New York also reported that at the end of the grant funding period, about 30 businesses were started, and that a total of 60 businesses were established through START-UP efforts, including the post-grant period.

Furthermore, state grantees noted that they considered a successful outcome of START-UP to be an informed decision *not* to start a business or pursue self-employment. Going through the discovery process led some people to conclude that entrepreneurship was not the right avenue for them, thereby enabling them to focus on wage employment opportunities.

The START-UP/USA data system did not collect information on the nature of the businesses. Success stories and anecdotal evidence revealed that the businesses covered numerous sectors, including automotive repair, automotive detailing, furniture manufacturing, online gift certificates, property management, home repair, dog

---

[22] The *Panel Survey of Entrepreneurial Dynamics* is conducted by the University of Michigan's Institute for Survey Research. More information can be found at http://www.psed.isr.umich.edu/psed/documentation.

[23] PSED results are from Gartner, William B., Shaver, Kelly G., Carter, Nancy M., Reynolds, and Paul D. *Handbook of Entrepreneurial Dynamics: The Process of Business Creation*. Thousand Oaks, CA: Sage Publications, 2004.

[24] Benus, Jacob, McConnell, Sheena, Belotti, Jeanne, Shen, Theodore, Fortson, Kenneth, Kahvecioblu, Daver. *Growing America Through Entrepreneurship: Findings from the Evaluation of Project GATE*. May 2008, P. 79.
http://wdr.doleta.gov/research/FullText_Documents/Findings%20from%20the%20Evaluation%20of%20Project%20GATE%20Report.pdf

[25] Milestones included 1) initiating a business plan, 2) completing a business plan, 3) completing a business feasibility study, 4) obtaining start-up funding, 5) creating a business, 6) filing state and federal taxes, 7) obtaining state and local business licenses, 8) making a sale, 9) expanding their business.

[26] Virginia Commonwealth University, *START-UP/USA Final Close-Out Report*, December 10, 2010.

kennels, photography, art, craft sales, restaurants and lodging, catering and food concessions, a variety of retail outlets, and internet-based and mail-order sales.

4. Evidence of Impacts on People with Disabilities

START-UP demonstrations assisted entrepreneurs from diverse backgrounds. START-UP/Alaska and START-UP/New York served all people interested in self-employment, with no regard to the nature of their disabilities. START-UP/Florida focused its efforts on individuals with developmental disabilities in Lakeland, disabled veterans in Jacksonville, and the general population of people with disabilities in Ft. Lauderdale/Miami. START/UP/Alaska reported that its referrals included individuals for whom frustrated caseworkers had "tried everything" in attempting to place them in wage employment. START-UP/USA reported on the primary diagnosis of 190[27] START-UP enrollees from the three sites. Almost half (47.4 percent) had physical impairments and 28.1 percent had cognitive or mental disabilities. The remainder had medical, visual, hearing impairments, or disabilities that were not disclosed.[28]

START-UP participants were asked at the time of enrollment if they were receiving SSI and/or SSDI. Forty-five individuals (23.2 percent) responded that they were receiving SSI; 67 (34.5 percent) were receiving SSDI. When asked if they were receiving health benefits, 133 (68.6 percent) responded affirmatively.[29] The START-UP/USA data system did not capture the status of benefit programs post-enrollment, and START-UP managers who were interviewed said they did not have statistics on the disability benefit status of START-UP enrollees after they launched their businesses. According to the information entered in the tracking database, a total of 43 participants received support from the projects related to Social Security work incentives, including writing a PASS. START-UP/USA reported data available from SSA revealed that only 103 (6.6 percent) of the total PASS plans by Social Security disability beneficiaries written in 2008 were individuals who had self-employment income.[30] The most recent Social Security data available reveal that in 2010, 83 out of 1,393 (6.0 percent) of Social Security disability beneficiaries with PASS plans had income from self-employment.[31]

The benefits to the participating individuals with disabilities reported by grant managers were increased income and increased self worth and satisfaction. Participants benefitted from being able to customize their employment to their disabilities and from having the freedom to use their talents and interests.

5. Evidence of Broader Impacts

In addition to the immediate outcomes of START-UP, the program has left a legacy among the grantees and the broader community. START-UP has continued in New York, and increased capacity exists in systems in Alaska and Florida. Furthermore, outcomes suggest that capacity developed through START-UP led to related initiatives that aim to improve the lives of people with disabilities.

a. Legacy of START-UP/USA

Although no longer funded by ODEP, VCU continues to make the START-UP/USA Web site available, including fact sheets, case studies, archived webcasts and online webinars. An important legacy of START-

---

[27] Not all of the 194 enrollees reported a primary diagnosis.

[28] Virginia Commonwealth University, *START-UP Final Close-Out Report*, December 10, 2010.

[29] The survey did not ask whether the source of health care was through Medicare, Medicaid, private or other sources. It is reasonable to expect that a substantial portion received Medicare and Medicaid, because SSDI and SSI beneficiaries qualify for these benefits.

[30] Retrieved from: http://www.ssa.gov/policy/docs/statcomps/ssi_asr/2008/sect07.html#table54.

[31] Retrieved from: http://www.ssa.gov/policy/docs/statcomps/ssi_asr/2010/sect07.html#table54.

UP/USA was informing SSA of the need for Limited Liability Companies (LLCs)[32] to be excluded under the PASS plan and then implementing an interpretation by the SSA reflecting this. START-UP/USA worked with START-UP/New York in developing an approach for using non-federally funded Individual Development Accounts (IDAs) to help finance business expenses. SSA agreed to an approach that permitted exclusion of those accounts from the SSI resource limits.[33] VCU and Griffin-Hammis are continuing to respond to requests for information and assistance submitted to the START-UP/USA website, and website visitors are continuing to download information and view the archived webinars. In the absence of funding, however, VCU is no longer able to tabulate statistics on visitors or use of the site.

START-UP/USA left a legacy far beyond the three demonstration states. Its staff provided policy samples, self-employment strategies, capacity building, and other information to VR personnel in Minnesota, California, New Mexico, Colorado, Rhode Island, Texas, Illinois, Michigan, Oregon, New Jersey, Iowa, New Hampshire, Nevada, Idaho, Arkansas, South Dakota, and other states. They were also instrumental in assisting Texas and Ohio in developing self-employment programs for people with disabilities.

b. Legacy of START-UP/New York

START-UP/New York has launched several offshoots of its program. First, it is continuing to support entrepreneurs with disabilities through collaboration between BBI; the South Side Innovation Center, a small business incubator in Syracuse, VR, and an SBDC. Second, *Inclusive Entrepreneurship*, the course developed collaboratively by BBI and the Whitman School of Management at Syracuse University, is now taken by graduate and undergraduate business and management majors. Third, START-UP/New York has been replicated in numerous locations (and further discussions are underway to create more branches both domestically and internationally). For example, it was replicated in Hunter College in New York City in a program to train rehabilitation counselors, and discussions are underway with Florida Atlantic University and with academics in Accra, Ghana. Furthermore, START-UP New York's Principal Investigator taught concepts from START-UP in Stellenbosch, South Africa, and BBI replicated START-UP in three more counties in New York through a Medicaid infrastructure grant. Fourth, BBI was awarded an SBA PRIME grant that integrated START-UP strategies with support for TANF recipients with disabilities. Fifth, START-UP/ New York collaborated with the Syracuse Cooperative Federal Credit Union to offer IDAs to START-UP grantees with matching funds provided by a foundation. The credit union provides basic financial counseling, with the expectation that successful entrepreneurs will bank with them as they become successful. START-UP/New York also produced several publications, including *Simply Speaking: Inclusive Entrepreneurship Guidelines for SBDC*

---

[32] Self-employed individuals often are advised from a business tax and liability perspective, and would prefer to form Limited Liability Companies (LLCs), sub-chapter S corporations or C corporations to protect their personal and family assets from potential lawsuits associated with their business. However, resources and assets of income from any for-profit corporation or any form of LLC are treated as personal resources subject to a $2,000 SSI personal resource limit in combination with the LLC's, member's or corporate stock holder's personal resources. If the limit is exceed, it causes the loss of SSI eligibility in all states (and loss of Medicaid in many states), whereas the resources and assets of sole proprietorships or partnerships are totally excluded by SSI and Medicaid. The business liability issue is that sole proprietorships or partnerships offer no liability protection for family and personal assets from business-related lawsuits. START-UP/USA worked with SSA to develop an interpretation that benefitted START-UP entrepreneurs seeking start-up funding from SSI's PASS. If an individual has a PASS, he or she may be able to exclude an LLC's entire net worth from the SSI $2,000 personal resource limit during the life of the PASS if the LLC structure is necessary to fulfill the plan. It is important to note that PASS is a limited duration work incentive, so when it comes to an end, the net worth (assets and resources) of the LLC would become a countable personal resource. The value of the business would likely be over the resource limit in any business that could produce an income for the owner significant enough to survive on without relying on SSI or Medicaid.

[33] START-UP/New York and START-UP/USA communicated with SSA via email to obtain clarification on circumstances under which a START-UP entrepreneur would be permitted to have a non-federal Individual Development Account (IDA) without jeopardizing SSI and Medicaid benefits. Although SSI does not exclude the resources of non-federal IDAs, both SSI and Medicaid do exclude the resources of federal Assets for Independence Act (AFIA) and TANF authorized/funded IDAs. Therefor the solution was to set the IDA up so it was trust-like in nature. The account required a signature by the IDA administrator as well as the individual for funds to be disbursed. And when the funds were dispersed, a check was made to the vendor of the particular item or service, the funds were not given to the individual. By doing that, the money the individual set aside in his or her IDA account was considered to be an excluded resource. SSA sent an email to START-UP staff stating, "if the funds are administered as described they can be excluded from income and resources and will therefore NOT affect an individual's receipt of SSI."

Advisors (2010)[34] and a chapter, "Inclusive Entrepreneurship" in *Academic Entrepreneurship and Community Engagement* (2011).[35]

c. Legacy of START-UP/Alaska

The management of START-UP/Alaska reported that employment and rehabilitation advisors in the state VR and employment security systems have been trained to support entrepreneurship for people with disabilities, and the know-how exists to enable entrepreneurship. Because of the networking among stakeholders in START-UP, working relationships now exist among involved agencies. A key legacy is attitudinal shifts and more knowledge and better understanding of what it takes to support small business development. The state's VR agency was also trained in and adopted discovery from START-UP. Furthermore, counselors from all of Alaska's SBDCs received training from START-UP/USA in discovery, customized self-employment and Quick-Launch business plan development in 2009. The Virtual Business Incubator successfully provided not only training, counseling and other supports to potential entrepreneurs in remote areas of the state, but also invaluable post-START-UP support to all 33 of those individuals who opened businesses. Alaska's Department of Disability and Senior Services put in a Medicaid waiver for the length of time self-employment supportive services could be provided. A self-employment policy summit was also held in February 2010. Participants included representatives from Alaska's divisions of VR, employment security (AJCs), behavioral health, public assistance and business partnerships. These state agencies were joined by representatives from the University of Alaska, including the Center for Human Development (the research contractor), the Center for Economic Development and SBDCs.

START-UP/Alaska also went on to secure complementary funding resources, much as START-UP/New York and START-UP/Florida did. Included were the Medicaid infrastructure grant, an economic development grant to the University of Alaska and a recent DOL ETA/ODEP Disability Employment Initiative (DEI) grant, which will expand self-employment efforts across the state. In addition, Alaska was awarded related grants, including one from SBA to develop a model for promoting the work of artists with disabilities and one from the Kessler Foundation to assist persons with traumatic brain injuries in pursuing self-employment. START-UP/Alaska was able to access funds from the Alaska Mental Health Trust Authority for capacity building and to support business startups.

d. Legacy of START-UP/Florida

Management of START-UP/Florida reported that silos have been bridged, and stakeholder agencies have developed working relationships. Key agencies previously operated in isolation. Now there are formal linkages between the organizations involved in supporting employment for people with disabilities. For instance, the Agency for Persons with Disabilities is now represented on the Board of Workforce Florida, Inc., which leads the state's workforce system. The department of VR now has trained Certified Business and Technical Assistance Consultants (CBTACs) to guide people with disabilities interested in developing small businesses. Another important legacy of START-UP/Florida is the inclusion of the BOSS manual as part of the high school curriculum to encourage self-employment for people with disabilities, distributed by the Florida Department of Education.

The state team at the University of South Florida and the state Department of Economic Opportunity (Formerly known as the Agency for Workforce Innovations) called on START-UP/ USA to explore reasonable outcome measures for AJCs considering the use of self-employment, and the workforce system went on to fund a trial of self-employment classes. The workforce system also funded a statewide demonstration project on self-employment that began operations in 2010. Further technical consultation was given by START-UP/USA to several school districts, most notably the Martin County school district, which adopted methods of assessment (discovery) and self-employment (the BOSS manual) to explore self-employment with transition-age youth. Numerous other school districts across Florida and the country have also requested information from START-UP/USA. The Florida department of VR was particularly supportive of START-UP/Florida and START-UP/USA and

---

[34] Published by *New York Makes Work Pay*, a statewide initiative intended to "dramatically improve the rate of employment among people with disabilities funded by the Center for Medicare and Medicaid Services.."

[35] Kingman, Bruce, Ed. *Academic Entrepreneurship and Community Engagement.* Edward Elgar, 2011.

concurrently re-wrote its self-employment policy to expressly expand self-employment and funded staff development and certification for its vendor network. Through 2010, more than 100 vendors had received certification in self-employment.[36]

Overall, the START-UP state demonstration projects used the influence of their grants to recommend and change policy. Figure 6 highlights examples of their impacts.

---

[36] Virginia Commonwealth University, *START-UP Final Close-Out Report*, December 10, 2010.

Figure 6: Highlights of START-UP Policy Influence

Grantee	START UP Policy Influences and Recommendations
START-UP/Alaska[37]	START-UP/Alaska's work resulted in changes to Alaska's Division of VR's policy on self-employment plans (34CFR§ 361.5(a) (16)) (extended closure period from 90 to 180 days, clarified funding for business start-up, incorporated the discovery process into the initial plan development, and included financial literacy requirements). Alaska's Employment Security Division's (ESD) policies will: • offer space to SBDC counselors and trainers at AJCs; • continue to use WIA funds when applicable for equipment and supplies necessary to complete training associated with development of a small business; • seek participation in the Self-Employment Assistance (SEA) program offered through the Unemployment Insurance (UI) program to allow the state to pay a "self-employed" allowance, instead of regular UI benefits, to help unemployed workers establish their businesses and become self-employed; and • seek a waiver to WIA Section 181(e) and 20 CFR 667.262, which prohibits the use of WIA funds for capitalization of businesses and similar activities that are not directly related to training for eligible individuals, so that allowance can be made for use of WIA funds for business capitalization costs.
START-UP/Florida[38]	The Agency for Persons with Disabilities (APD) submitted a formal request for manual revisions that will allow supported self-employment to become an authorized service available through the Medicaid waiver. VR has worked cooperatively with APD to expand the role of VR's CBTACs to be an authorized provider for APD customers pursuing self-employment. APD policy uses VR's supported self-employment manual as a guide for delivery of services, including a system of provider reimbursement based on benchmarks.
START-UP/New York[39]	The Syracuse University/Whitman School of Management adopted the *Inclusive Entrepreneurship* course and components of the discovery model as a new core focus of the entrepreneurship teaching it offers through its curriculum and the services it provides through its business incubator in the community. The New York State Senate introduced two bills, S.6095 and S. 6096, on January 4, 2012, aimed at dramatically expanding entrepreneurship opportunities for people with disabilities.
START-UP/USA[40]	START-UP/ USA requested clarification from SSA and implemented an interpretation by the SSA that LLCs can be excluded under the work incentive PASS. Worked with START-UP/New York to develop a policy of excluding non-federally funded IDAs from the SSI resource limits, which was accepted by SSA.

---

[37] Saunders, Rich. *Alaska Works Self-employment Project – START-UP/Alaska Final Report.* Alaska Governor's Council on Disabilities & Special Education, December 2010.

[38] From *Action Plan to Address Recommendations Made By NDIF For Implementation by START-UP/Florida State Steering Committee,* April 2009, attached to *START-UP/Florida Quarterly Progress Report,* March 31, 2009.

[39]Onondaga County in partnership with the Burton Blatt Institute and Whitman School of Management.

of Syracuse University. *Inclusive Entrepreneurship*, November 17, 2010. (Final Report of START-UP/New York.)

[40] Virginia Commonwealth University, *START-UP/USA Final Close-Out Report*, December 10, 2010.

4. Self-employment success stories from the Demonstrations

As discussed previously, state demonstration sites assisted 194 entrepreneurs with disabilities in pursuing self-employment. The following success stories anecdotally illustrate the variety of outcomes and impacts of the programs.

START-UP/Alaska Entrepreneurs

Elizabeth's Story—Occupational Therapist

Elizabeth, who has a visual disability, had a longstanding relationship with the Division of Vocational Rehabilitation (DVR) and had received assistive devices, including a computer to support wage employment as an occupational therapist (OT). Elizabeth's self-employment goal was to start an OT private practice. She had more than 16 years' experience as an OT in various settings, including schools, nursing homes, hospitals and community agencies. Elizabeth decided to open a practice focusing on children with autism and sensory-processing disabilities.

Her business gave her the control and flexibility that she needed, while also providing accommodations for her visual disability. A physical therapist and a speech and language pathologist offered to share their treatment space and equipment. Elizabeth also needed to purchase evaluation materials and additional equipment, such as a swing, spinner board, tilt board, sensory-tactile items and a sound system. Furthermore, she needed assistive technology (AT) to accommodate her disability, including a closed-circuit TV-camera system. Using the closed-circuit TV system, Elizabeth would be able to videotape the children in her practice and use the video to closely view her OT evaluations and treatment sessions. She also needed an AT device that could read journals and reports aloud, allowing Elizabeth to stay current in her practice.

START-UP/Alaska assisted Elizabeth in developing her business plan and financial projections, as well as accessing additional funding from the Alaska Mental Health Trust Authority's microenterprise fund, which was approved. This funding also provided a match to the funds Alaska's DVR was willing to provide for the business start-up.

Jacquelyn's Story—Dog Breeding and Grooming

Jacquelyn made a life for herself in Alaska living off the land. After the Exxon Valdez oil spill, Jacquelyn went to Valdez to volunteer cleaning animals. She was one of the few individuals who could keep the baby sea otters alive. From this experience, Jacquelyn realized that she has a special gift for caring for small and fragile animals. A few years later, Jacquelyn purchased several Yorkshire terriers and a miniature poodle and began breeding them. Initially, this was only for pleasure, but eventually she began to sell the puppies of the registered parent dogs.

Jacquelyn has a disability that sometimes limits her strength, and she was realistic that being in her 50s, she would not be able to live off the land indefinitely. She needed a reliable income. Jacquelyn was referred to START-UP/Alaska by her counselor at the Alaska DVR. Subsequently, she took several classes offered by the Fairbanks SBDC. With the information she learned, she wrote a draft business plan. In it, Jacquelyn was able to articulate all the details of breeding and operations of her planned kennel, which would include indoor-outdoor runs, a security camera system for night monitoring, and equipment and supplies to care for her dogs, allowing her to do most of her own veterinary care.

Jacquelyn agreed to be the first client to try counseling via the Internet. START-UP virtual incubator counselors assisted her with the financial management aspects of the plan and helped her to find funding for the supplies and equipment she needed. The plan's financial projections showed that her kennel could bring in a reliable income to sustain Jacquelyn in her chosen lifestyle. With a sound business plan, DVR and the Alaska Mental Health Trust Authority's microenterprise grant program funded her start-up expenses, and Jacquelyn became a successful entrepreneur who is self-sufficient. With her new equipment and supplies, Jacquelyn was able to increase her breeding to meet the market demand and plans to add grooming to her services. START-UP/Alaska helped her to customize her business to fit her own physical abilities and needs.

Roberta's Story—Self-Employment Counseling

Roberta was a communications and marketing consultant until a workplace accident left her with a traumatic brain injury and a visual impairment. After recovery, she realized that she needed a flexible schedule due to her disabilities, which included migraine headaches. The migraines made it necessary for Roberta to build in extra time for project completion and did not allow her to finish work with short deadlines. These concerns impacted her ability to hold a wage employment position.

Roberta began pursuing options at the YWCA, where she connected with counselors at its Alaska Microenterprise Incubation (AMI) center. The AMI center provides women who work from home offices a chance to access a shared-use, private office space, away from children and the duties at home. Run by the YWCA Anchorage Women's Finance Program, the center also offers workshops, seminars and other training primarily for women. Roberta audited the AMI center's intensive three-day training program and established a relationship with the staff. She also took the center's class on starting a business and considered the loan-guarantee program. After Roberta disclosed her disability, the AMI center referred her to START-UP/Alaska in June 2008 for information about available supports and funding.

The START-UP facilitator and the DVR counselor worked with Roberta to help her understand that she needed assistive technology (AT) to accommodate her visual impairment. Roberta chose to access services from DVR and tribal VR on a plan to assess self-employment as an employment option. Together, the two agencies provided funding to support her business start-up. The two agencies also provided funding for a 12-week small business training course through the SBDC and bought office equipment needed while she investigated the feasibility of a consulting firm. Roberta submitted a grant request to the Alaska Mental Health Trust's microenterprise fund for the balance of funding needed to start her business. Roberta was awarded the grant and enrolled in two desktop publishing classes.

As a result of this process, Roberta realized that there were other potential business owners who would need to submit business plans to VR programs and for funding, but who didn't have her skills in developing a plan. She applied for and became a DVR vendor to help others with disabilities become self-employed. Roberta is now assisting DVR clients who want to become self-employed, as well as serving clients from the business community. By combining her business skills and passion, she is now able to help more people become small business owners.

START-UP/Florida Entrepreneurs

Ren's Story—Fly Fishing Equipment

Ren connected with START-UP/Florida when the SBDC suggested that he attend a training session it was offering on self-employment for individuals with disabilities. The training was sponsored by START-UP/Florida and START-UP/USA and held at the AJC in Lakeland, Florida. After listening to the presentation, he realized that he could pursue selling handmade bamboo fly rods, this combining a personal hobby and his need for employment.

The first step was to conduct a feasibility study. He then developed his business plan with input from START-UP/Florida and START-UP/USA. Once the business plan was completed, it was submitted to VR for review. Based on this review, he received funding for start-up costs and opened for business on November 2, 2007 specializing in the production and sales of hand-crafted, split-cane bamboo fly rods and handmade fly reels. START-UP/Florida also assisted him in writing a PASS, which was approved for an 18-month period.

Greg's Story—Automotive Repair

For 35 years, Greg and his father owned and operated an auto detailing and minor repair shop. After his father passed away, the business gradually decreased, and Greg experienced a debilitating back injury. As a result, he was unable to manage the physical demands of the business and sales dropped. Greg wanted to work. However, he did not want to close the business that he had built with his father. Since Greg owned the property, he decided to rent parking spaces to supplement the detail work. Because the business was not turning a profit, he applied for and began receiving SSDI benefits to supplement his wife's earnings and to cover their basic monthly bills.

In March 2008, Greg learned about START-UP/New York from another participant. The program's Business Navigator supported Greg through a process of identifying and inventorying his strengths and conditions for employment. Greg began exploring how his current strengths could fit into an auto detail and minor repair business, while at the same time, identifying ways to provide accommodations for certain tasks. Through brainstorming, the idea emerged to build having employees into the business model and to diversify services. As his business ideas developed, Greg realized that he needed to complete a feasibility study. He had concerns that the business would not be able to bring in enough sales to pay for an employee.

Greg was referred to the local Work Incentive Planner[41] who specialized in understanding benefits related to self-employment. Greg received some preliminary information about potential changes to his benefits if he decided to pursue growing his business. The next step was to include the SBDC, which was facilitated by the START-UP/New York Business Navigator. The SBDC counselor provided Greg support and structure for gathering the information needed to complete his feasibility study. During this process, Greg was encouraged to reach out and utilize his well-established network within the local auto industry to gather information on industry standards, trends and opportunities. Through this research, Greg identified a local auto mechanic who was interested in teaming up with him to offer state inspections and repairs at his shop. As Greg began to gather the feasibility information, it became clear to him that a market was still available in his community. He also realized that his business could be financially viable even with employees.

Once Greg completed the discovery and feasibility phases, he felt confident about making a decision to build his business to a profitable level. Based on information he had gathered, Greg decided to continue offering detailing services and hire an employee to do the bulk of the work. To reach this goal, Greg needed a business plan to include the critical details of growing his business. He again talked with START-UP/New York, which recommended that he apply for assistance from the Inclusive Entrepreneurship class at Syracuse University's Whitman School of Business. As a part of the class, students work in groups to support an entrepreneur with a disability. Together, Greg and the group identified four outcomes to include marketing segmentation; redesigning business cards, fliers and marketing communications; drafting a letter to potential fleet agency managers; and compilation and completion of a business plan. Over time, Greg implemented the first portion of his business plan, which included hiring an employee to perform auto detailing and minor repairs.

Stella's Story—Restaurant

Stella had been unemployed due to numerous foot surgeries and a lupus diagnosis. One day she went to the Women Igniting the Spirit of Entrepreneurship Center at Syracuse University, where she met a number of women who shared a variety of resources available to her as a minority woman. Upon further exploration, it became clear that Stella would like to start a taco restaurant.

Stella was referred to START-UP/New York and met with the local Certified Work Incentives Planner. Stella attended a monthly workshop that provided an overview of available work incentives including a PASS. Stella

---

[41] SSA provided Community Work Incentive Coordinators (CWICs) in 102 locations around the country to assist with work incentive planning through its Work Incentive Planning and Assistance project (http://www.ssa.gov/work/wipafactsheet.html).

received $785/month of SSDI. With an approved PASS, she could set aside $765 per month of her SSDI monthly benefit to pay for start-up expenses. After this was set aside, she would receive $761 per month of SSI and New York's State Supplement to cover her monthly living expenses. The Work Incentives Planner assisted Stella in completing the PASS application and submitting it to SSA once she had her business plan completed, a required step for a PASS with a self-employment work goal. At the close of START-UP funding, Stella had located the ideal location and was refining her business plan.

MJ's Story—Photography

MJ's mental health disability affected his ability to maintain and advance in employment. After years of experimenting with medications and counseling, he was able to stabilize his condition. Given his natural talent and interest in the arts, MJ determined photography and painting would be the best fit. While searching for help, MJ learned about START-UP/New York from the SBDC. He contacted the START-UP/New York facilitator, who then helped him to refine his business plan and to secure start-up funding. In April 2008, MJ was referred to the local Work Incentives Planner who helped him rewrite his PASS application. Eventually, MJ was able to accumulate enough start-up funds for initial operating expenses and photography equipment to enable him to launch a business.

5. Policy and Systems Barriers and Facilitators of the Tested Interventions

Expected Barriers

In developing their projects, demonstration grantees faced a number of barriers associated with local operating conditions, the conflict between vision and reality that all systems change endeavors encounter, and barriers that could be attributed to federal and state program policies.

Attitudes and Views. Each of the START-UP demonstrations began with an exploration of which organizations should be called upon to play a role in improving self-employment opportunities for people with disabilities. In most instances the key agencies that participated in START-UP (workforce development, VR and SBDCs) are separate entities that have their own priorities and performance expectations. While all have missions that can benefit people with disabilities, they routinely have not joined together to develop self-employment options for people with disabilities. All of the sites formed consortia, and there was variation in the length of time it took for agencies to cooperate and constructively pursue collaborative actions toward START-UP's goals. Attitudes, beliefs, and views that self-employment was not possible or appropriate for people with disabilities was an obstacle to progress that grantees had to overcome with communication and education.

Inconsistent Expectations. A consistent vision was not held by all parties involved as to what outcomes should be expected. One individual in a leadership position felt that the agencies bearing the funding burden to support self-employment should be able to limit self-employment aspirations to entrepreneurs with the greatest earnings potential. Other individuals expressed views that an improved quality of life is a worthwhile outcome, and that if self-employment moved a person from an existing job environment that paid low wages and did not take advantage of their capabilities, the outcome should be considered positive regardless of income potential. This tension over what outcomes are reasonable remained among some of the consortia members over time.

Know-how. All START-UP grantees mentioned that key players involved in service delivery generally had no formal training or depth of knowledge in what it takes to start a small business and what kinds of supports people with disabilities would need to succeed as entrepreneurs. Grantees spent considerable time and effort preparing and securing resources to assist grantees in entrepreneurship. A substantial amount of time was also spent identifying barriers and obstacles to self-employment on an individual participant level and on a systems level, including service providers. Each grantee had to conduct an exploration and analysis of the resources and systems available. Staff training and cross-system collaboration and capacity building remained a significant challenge.

Inconsistent Performance Expectations. Support for entrepreneurship involved departments of VR, funded through the U.S. Department of Education; AJCs, funded by DOL; disability benefits, funded through the SSA; and resources and training, offered by SBDCs and funded through the SBA. Each of these organizations has different performance expectations under the Government Performance and Results Act (GPRA). Performance goals that strive to reduce dependency on government assistance benefits quickly are at odds with self-employment and entrepreneurship, which take time to develop. Except for SBA programs, none of the other stakeholders has explicit performance goals in support of self-employment. It is an acceptable outcome, but because of the lack of knowledge in assisting people with disabilities to pursue self-employment and the time it takes to develop a business, support for entrepreneurship remains a secondary priority for systems focused on achievement of employment outcomes.

Policies that Lead to Financial Disincentives for Self-Employment. People with disabilities are concerned about the risk of losing disability benefits because of earnings from a small business. Government cash assistance programs provide a standard of living just above poverty, and earnings from self-employment can jeopardize eligibility for benefits, such as SSI and Medicaid, or reduce benefit amounts. Grantees felt overwhelmingly that such a low standard of living is not an incentive to remain on cash assistance benefits. Yet they observed that some people with disabilities feared that earnings from self-employment might not be sufficient to make up for reduced or lost cash assistance and health benefits. Such concerns had to be addressed by grantees, and these concerns prevented some people with disabilities from pursuing self- employment.

One grantee explored using IDAs to generate cash reserves for businesses, but found that participants must have earned income to qualify for matching IDA funds. The business launch phase is the worst time to expect earnings, but also the time that funds are most needed. One grantee was able to obtain matching funds through a foundation instead of through participants' earned income, but was unable to use the foundation grant's funds because IDAs require matching funds from earned income.

Complicated Work Incentives. Federal work-incentive policies are geared toward wage employment and are very complicated relative to funding self-employment. Start-Up/USA spent considerable effort exploring this issue and counseling people with disabilities on how to work within the system. Although this obstacle was overcome in many instances for START-UP participants, the effort and resources to deal with it is a barrier for agencies and people with disabilities. Further, the amount of savings permitted to retain SSI benefits is set at $2,000, which is a very small cash reserve for a nascent business.

Funding Challenges. Policies and funding in VR, Social Security, and Medicaid are geared toward wage employment and pose barriers to self-employment. VR programs offer limited funding, if any, for discovery. VR funding may be inadequate to cover initial start-up and ongoing costs. Social Security and Medicaid income and asset limits challenge entrepreneurs during the critical start-up phase of a business.

Some interview respondents expressed concern about ongoing funding to continue support for self- employment. In observing the legacies of START-UP, greater success and continuity of support is observed in demonstrations sites where resources from universities, grants and foundations were used to continue START-UP efforts. The ongoing commitment and expertise of BBI at Syracuse University and the Alaska Mental Health Trust Authority in Alaska provided an ongoing funding stream to continue and expand services in support of entrepreneurship for people with disabilities. The absence of such expertise and non-government resources could pose a barrier to other locations seeking to support entrepreneurship.

Unexpected Barriers

Participants' Views and Attitudes. Grantees reported that some people with disabilities held limiting views that prevented them from considering self-employment as a possibility. They had spent their lives being told "you can't" and did not believe it would be possible for them to own a business or become self-employed. Grantees expressed how gratifying it was for participants and for them to assist someone who never thought it would be possible to own a business, especially people whose talents and skills were underutilized in jobs with little to no potential for growth and advancement. Grantees also noted that in some instances, people spent two or three years in the system and were declared totally "unemployable" by the SSA. Because of this, they were not inclined to seek self-employment or any employment for that matter. Clearly, having been declared unemployable is not an incentive to seek employment. Overall, grantees spent more effort than they expected in addressing such concerns of participants.

Language and Communication. By bringing together stakeholders from the business and social service communities, grantees found that language could be a barrier. Economic development partners like SBDCs and business incubators tend to use a different vocabulary, one related to market analysis, return on investment and business feasibility, than people with disabilities and service agencies, who tend to converse in terms focused on public benefits and work incentives. The term "mainstream," for instance, has very different meanings to the business community and to the disability community. Thus, START-UP managers had to be sensitive to communication issues in managing the collaborative process.[42]

---

[42] Shaheen, Gary and Mintz, Jason. *Mapping the Barriers and Facilitators to Self-Employment for People with Disabilities Living in Onondaga County, NY.* September 14, 2007.

6. RECOMMENDATIONS FOR THE FUTURE

The emerging and growing promise of self-employment, documented by the individual and systemic outcomes achieved by START-UP's three funded demonstration projects and national technical assistance center, raise the bar of expectations for all relevant stakeholders: government, the business community, service delivery systems, and people with disabilities and their families.

The START-UP initiative set a new conceptual framework that recognizes the creative spirit and capacity of people with disabilities to be a part of the economic mainstream and contribute to America's long-standing spirit of entrepreneurism. With access to appropriate supports and improved coordination of multiple, publicly funded service-delivery systems, people with disabilities can successfully pursue self-employment as a choice to produce income, create jobs, reduce their reliance on public benefits, advance their economic self-sufficiency, and improve the quality of their lives. As such, self-employment should be among the national disability employment policy priorities.

To produce a long-term return on investment of the $5,000,000 expended on the START-UP initiative, recommendations that provide a road map for sustainable, systematic change at the local, state and federal levels are outlined below. The recommendations focus on policy and practice to accomplish three main objectives:

1. Align policy across systems to reduce and eliminate barriers to individual exploration of entrepreneurial goals that encourage income production and advancement of economic self-sufficiency;

2. Promote cross-system collaboration and braiding of resources to invest in business start-up and job creation for individuals with disabilities; and

3. Encourage public- and private-sector investment in, and purchase of, products and services offered by businesses owned by people with disabilities.

Policy Alignment

Performance measures drive system behavior. Current federal performance measures for the public workforce system do not account for activities at a state or local level that encourage and support self-employment outcomes. If self-employment is not a stated and measured outcome, agencies are not likely to give it priority and visibility. Reflecting this, the first recommendation is as follows:

Recommendation 1: *Consider requiring state and local workforce investment boards to collect exit data on self-employment outcomes and business start-ups with the number of jobs created. This would necessitate modifying common performance measures to include a new set of separate indicators for self-employment outcomes and wage employment outcomes, as well as milestones that support self-employment outcomes, such as discovery and business plan development.*

RSA and SSA do collect information on self-employment for exiters of their respective VR programs and work incentive programs. However, the proportion of exiters in self-employment is very low, much lower than the incidence of self-employment in the general labor force. To improve the number of exiters in self-employment, a second recommendation is as follows:

Recommendation 2: *Explore the possibility of having state VR agencies report annually to RSA on indicators of expanded capacity and support of customers with disabilities who are interested in pursuing entrepreneurial goals. To facilitate this, self-employment outcomes for VR, SSDI and SSI exiters should have a benchmark, such as the rate of self- employment in the general labor force. Benchmarks would also need to be established for critical groups, such as youth in transition and people with prior employment experience.*

In general, the underutilization of PASS and other work incentives, as well as their complexity and cumbersome approval processes, may necessitate a rethinking and redesign. Reflecting this, a third recommendation is as follows:

> **Recommendation 3**: *Seek ways to simplify the PASS process and make it friendlier to self-employment. For instance, SSA could require SSI recipients to opt out, rather than into, the design and creation of a PASS. This would require providing benefits advisement customized to individual needs that discusses the choice of self-employment as a work objective, provides linkages to supports and services that help explore entrepreneurship goals, and includes benefits planning assistance.*

Restrictions on savings and earnings for individuals receiving SSI benefits make it more difficult for an individual with a disability to accumulate funds needed to start and sustain a new business. PESS is an underutilized Social Security work incentive that does not count certain resources in determining continuing eligibility for SSI. Confusion exists as to whether SSI resource exclusion for PESS applies to business assets owned by an LLC. In response to the confusion, a fourth recommendation is as follows:

> **Recommendation 4**: *Review legislation and SSA policies and guidance concerning income, resources and assets, in order to make them friendlier to self-employment. As part of this, SSA could issue guidance to its field offices, clarifying that assets owned by an LLC would not be counted in determining continuing eligibility for SSI to further encourage self-employment as an approach to advancing self-sufficiency.*

Several state and local agencies play an important role in preparing youth for employment and in providing services that prepare people with disabilities for employment. RSA-funded VR agencies have policies supporting wage employment but not policies tailored to self-employment. The low rate of RSA case closures resulting in self-employment indicates that the policy infrastructure does not exist to support it as an outcome in state and local agencies. Policy alignment is needed at the federal and state levels to cultivate a nationwide infrastructure to produce higher rates of self-employment. Reflecting this, a fifth recommendation is as follows:

> **Recommendation 5**: *Federal and state agencies could work to better align policies in support of self-employment for people with disabilities. For instance, RSA could articulate policies specific to self-employment, including curricula for youth approaching transition, certification, and training for providers to guide people with disabilities in developing small businesses, and financial support for the small business development process, including discovery, business plan development, and implementation of business plans. In order to ensure effectiveness, RSA policy guidance could include cooperation and collaboration with other agencies that play a key role in self-employment, including SBDCs, Social Security, Medicaid, and AJCs. Policies of all involved agencies would need to be aligned to recognize that a self-employment outcome requires more time and specialized support than a wage employment outcome.*

Cross System Collaboration

Lessons learned from the START-UP initiative document the challenges of multiple fragmented service delivery systems that make it more difficult at a community level for an individual with a disability to access needed services and supports to advance self-employment objectives. The lack of cross-system collaboration at the federal level contributes to this lack of cross-system collaboration at the local level. To improve cross-system collaboration, a sixth recommendation is as follows:

> **Recommendation 6**: *Consider the establishment of, through a vehicle such as an Executive Order or Congressional directive, a time-limited work group or advisory committee that would be charged with setting an action-oriented agenda for improving cross-system collaboration to support self-employment for individuals with disabilities. The work group would include decision makers from the SBA, RSA, ETA, Office of Special Education and Rehabilitation Services, SSA, Economic Development Administration, and Centers for Medicare and Medicaid services. The work group could be facilitated by ODEP. At a minimum, this collaborative group would develop shared goals and propose policy changes. These would include, but not be limited to, proposing legislative and regulatory change, issuing policy guidance, and developing a budget and timeline for achievement.*

One of the consistent observations of START-UP grantees was the lack of knowledge among counselors within the public workforce system about resources available to help job seekers interested in self-employment as an alternative to wages, and the lack of an explicit mission to support such ambitions. To resolve this problem, seventh and eighth recommendations are as follows:

> **Recommendation 7:** *Consider developing a cooperative agreement for collaboration between ODEP and SBA and ODEP and RSA that promotes counselor education about self-employment as a career goal for individuals with disabilities and provides linkages to agency resources to customize assistance.*

> **Recommendation 8:** *Study the establishment of an entrepreneurship innovation fund with resources set aside by RSA, ETA, SSA, SBA, and EDA.* This competitive fund would be used for grants demonstrating the commitment of multiple service delivery systems at a state level to coordinate resources and create a unified pathway geared toward entrepreneurship for people both with and without disabilities. The grants would support staff training and development, private sector matched investment, and streamlined service delivery systems.

Public-Private Sector Investment

The federal government and state governments are major purchasers of goods and services. Requirements of government procurement mandate that a prime contract includes a small business subcontracting plan. Most large businesses now have supplier diversity programs and set annual goals for purchasing from minority-owned businesses. But, little has been done proactively by government to build the capacity of small businesses that are owned by people with disabilities to compete and be valued subcontractors in the public or private sector. The U.S. Business Leadership Network (USBLN) Disability Supplier Diversity Program (DSDP) has created a certification program and database for disability-owned businesses, which is a step forward. Reflecting this, a ninth recommendation is as follows:

> **Recommendation 9:** *SBA, ETA, and ODEP could consider working together to improve coordination between SBDCs nationwide and AJCs that provide training and technical assistance to individuals with disabilities who want to start and grow small businesses. The goal of this coordination would be to improve the ability of individuals with disabilities to compete for government procurement as prime contractors for small business set-asides and as subcontractors in larger competitions. Annual plans and reporting requirements could be developed to describe capacity-building activities and report quantitative outcomes.*

Access to capital is always a challenge for potential entrepreneurs. Financial institutions under the Community Reinvestment Act (CRA) have obligations to serve disadvantaged, low-income individuals in their geographic areas. Persons with disabilities are not a specifically-targeted class. To address this issue, a tenth recommendation is as follows:

> **Recommendation 10:** *Consider clarifying by proposed rule changes stipulating that under the CRA, financial institutions must document their lending practices in support of small business start-ups owned by persons with disabilities.*

Future Research

The START-UP initiative did not provide sufficient time to investigate long-term outcomes and critical barriers to success. More needs to be learned about effective cross-system collaboration and capacity building to advance entrepreneurship goals for people with disabilities. For example, strategies need to be investigated that could streamline financing and eliminate exclusions to cash and health care benefits and more needs to be learned about the barriers to access to capital for small business start-up and growth. Furthermore, start-ups need to be followed longitudinally to assess longer-range economic and individual outcomes and to identify significant barriers to sustainability and growth. At present, there is no centralized federal body that advances entrepreneurship for people with disabilities, and relevant agencies do not have current research initiatives on the subject. Reflecting this, an eleventh and twelfth recommendation are as follows:

Recommendation 11: *Explore establishing a National Resource Center to Promote Entrepreneurship for People with Disabilities . This Center would conduct relevant policy research and investigate systems transformation issues as well as support training and provide technical assistance to states and the public workforce system to advances self-employment outcomes for people with disabilities. An annual report would update all relevant stakeholders, including the White House and Congress, on barriers and facilitators to self- employment and quantitative indicators of progress to date.*

Recommendation 12: *The research budgets of relevant participating agencies (for instance, ETA, RSA, SBA, SSA and EDA) could set priorities to increase knowledge and understanding of effective policy and practices to support entrepreneurs with disabilities.*

7. CONCLUSION

The strength of the START-UP initiative was to begin to document the potential benefits of cross-system collaboration and the increased support of individuals with disabilities interested in self-employment. The proposed recommendations in this report focus on resource coordination and policy alignment to shape individual and system-wide behavior. A continued investment in research, capacity building and knowledge translation can empower people with disabilities to build self-sufficiency and pay an important role in our nation's economic recovery.

8. Appendices

Appendix 1. START-UP/USA WEBCAST SERIES

Each year of the project, START-UP/USA produced and streamed live webcasts for a total of 19 webcasts produced. These webcasts continue to be available through VCU's support even though funding has ended for the project.

Webcasts were offered as a series to our stakeholders but they could also register for these as individual events. A total of **2,545** individuals participated in the webcasts during the course of the project. In 2007, there were a total of **996** participants; in 2008, **840**; and in 2009, **709** participants.

YEAR ONE LIVE WEBCAST SERIES

A Self-Employment Success Story
Number of Participants: 132

Entrepreneurship Resources and Services
Number of Participants: 178

Family Support of Self-Employment
Number of Participants: 138

Developing A Business Plan for Self-Employment
Number of Participants: 130

PASS for Self-Employment
Number of Participants: 131

Self-Employment for Disabled Veterans
Number of Participants: 155

Self-Employment: Vision, Partnerships and Creative Funding
Number of Participants: 132

YEAR TWO LIVE WEBCAST SERIES

Community Small Business Development Resources
Number of Participants: 134

Medicaid Waivers: A Tool for Self-Employment
Number of Participants: 157

Community Rehabilitation Providers & Creative Funding for Self-Employment
Number of Participants: 122

Small Business Development Center - Business Planning and Implementation
Number of Participants: 146

Family Support and Self-Employment
Number of Participants: 132

Microloans & Small Business Loans
Number of Participants: 149

YEAR THREE LIVE WEBCAST SERIES

Negotiation Strategies for Business Owners & Promoters
Number of Participants: 121

The Customized Self-Employment Model
Number of Participants: 116

Inclusive Entrepreneurship
Number of Participants: 114

Current Research in Self-Employment
Number of Participants: 118

Three Models of Self-employment
Number of Participants: 125

The Financial Side of Self-Employment
Number of participants: 115

WEBCAST ARCHIVES

After the live events, all webcasts were made available free of charge on the project's website. A review of the online statistics reveals that the archives have been used by **11,276 visitors** with a total of **17,442 page views**. The availability of the archives has significantly increased the reach of the project.

Year One Webcast Archive - Available Online at:
http://www.start-up-usa.biz/training/archivedWebcasts.cfm?yr=2007#info

Year Two Webcast Archive - Available Online at:
http://www.start-up-usa.biz/training/archivedWebcasts.cfm?yr=2008#info

Year Three Webcast Archive - Available Online at:
http://www.start-up-usa.biz/training/archivedWebcasts.cfm?yr=2009

Appendix 2. START-UP/USA FACT SHEETS

Eighteen fact sheets and other resources were made available online during the project. These fact sheets continue to be available at: http://www.start-up-usa.biz/resources/index.cfm . A review of the web statistics shows that **12,866 individuals** accessed the fact sheets during the length of the project with a total of **28,576 page views**.

Project Fact Sheets:

1. START-UP/USA Self-Employment Q and A: Braiding and Blending Funding for Business Start-Up

2. Self-Employment Q and A: Assistance not Assessment: Getting at the Heart of Small Business Feasibility

3. Self-Employment Q and A: Small Business Development Centers

4. Self-Employment Q and A: An Analysis of Self-Employment Outcomes within the Vocational Rehabilitation System

5. Self-Employment Q and A: Low Cost/No Cost Marketing Strategies for Small Businesses

6. Self-Employment Q and A: Selecting a Business Structure

7. Plan to Achieve Self Support and Self-Employment

8. Self-Employment Q and A: Information on Entrepreneurship for Youth with Disabilities

9. Self-Employment Q and A: Discovery

10. Person-First Considerations for Generating Small Business Ideas

11. Self-Employment Q and A: Frequently Asked Questions from Families

12. Medicaid Home and Community Based Services

13. Disabled Veterans and Self-Employment

14. Community Resources

15. Successful Entrepreneurs with Disabilities Speak Out

16. Accessing VR Services

17. Develop a Business Plan

18. Self-Employment

Appendix 3. START-UP/USA SELF-EMPLOYMENT ONLINE COURSE

A total of **335** individuals participated in the online course that was developed by the project from April 2009 through November 2010. The course was offered eight times during this time period. Of the 335 individuals who were enrolled in the online course, a total of **205 were individuals with disabilities** who received the course free of charge.

The last section of the course was specifically offered to individuals who belong to the MS Society, and a total of 75 participants were enrolled. Based on the feedback from the participants, the MS Society began offering the online course to its participants throughout the U.S. beginning in 2011.

The course is covering these important topics on self-employment and more:

- Strategies for Exploration and the Discovery Process
- Writing a Business Plan
- Conducting a Feasibility Study
- Accessing Community Supports
- Identifying Funding
- Using Work Incentives

Lesson One: Self-Employment Overview

Lesson Two: Social Security Work Incentives, Medicaid Waivers, and Self-Employment

Lesson Three: Accessing Support Services from Vocational Rehabilitation and Community Rehabilitation Programs

Lesson Four: Community Supports for Self-Employment

Lesson Five: Quick-Launch Business Start-Up

Participating Agencies	
Alaska Division of Vocational Rehabilitation	Minot State University
California Dept. of Rehabilitation	Missouri Vocational Rehabilitation
Chesterfield Vocational Services	National Organization on Disability
Community Integrated Services	New Directions
Community Opportunities	Northeast Michigan Comm. Mental Health
County of Summit Board of MRDD	Ohio Rehabilitation Services Commission
DARS/Division for Blind Services Texas	Oklahoma Dept. of Rehabilitation Services
DHS - Vocational Rehabilitation	American Job Centers
DisAbility Resource Center	Progressive Community Services
EmployAbility	Prince George County Public Schools
Employment Resources, Inc.	Radford University
Good will SWPA	REACH-Inc.
Graves Consulting & Transition Services	Ridge Meadows Association for Community Living
Independent Abilities Center	The Cerebral Palsy Center
Idaho Division of Vocational Rehabilitation	The Polus Center
Illinois Assistive Technology Program	University of Massachusetts, Institute for Community
Independent Living Resources	Inclusion, Boston
Jackson County Developmental Center, Inc.	United Cerebral Palsy of Michigan
Jennifer Logan Rehabilitation Services	Work-Able, Inc.
Kaposia, Inc.	The Jewish Disability Empowerment Center
Lane Community College	

The online course served as the foundation for the development of Florida's online Certified Business and Technical Assistance Consultant (CBTAC) Certification for self-employment and the FL-CBTAC Re-certification Courses. In addition, this course was being replicated in both Texas and Ohio beginning in 2011. The appendix includes the outline for the course that is now available through Virginia Commonwealth University in collaboration with Griffin-Hammis, LLC and the Center for Social Capital.

www.ingramcontent.com/pod-product-compliance
Lightning Source LLC
Chambersburg PA
CBHW080627290526
45790CB00007B/2958